Mourning After the Storm

Nathan Ross

CONTENTS

Dedication..1

Acknowledgements 2

Disclaimer..4

Foundation...6

Extremes 10

Pressure..13

Ally 21

Calm 27

Hope..31

Fear...36

Race...39

Community...41

Vacation..48

Special 53

Creative... 59

Educate... 65

Evil..74

Point of No Return...82

Snap 85

Shelter 95

Transition..100

Confusion 104

Foster 109

Help...112

Test..115

Break...119

Normal..125

Trial 128

Disrupt...133

Integration 137

Reflection..148

Autonomy 153

Competence 155

Identity 161

Individualism..172

Wisdom 184

Timeline of Events 191

Resources..192

Notes...193

DEDICATION

In deepest memory of Larry and Gary Bass. The love you two gave, in such a brief time, was felt by all who were fortunate enough to know you. It is because of the sacrifice that you both made that I am able to have the life that I do. You will never be forgotten.

This book is also dedicated to Jerry and Catina. You both helped me make it through the darkest time in my life and gave me the strength to keep going every day. I don't know how I would have survived without the two of you. No amount of thanks will ever express how much I love and cherish you both. Thank you.

ACKNOWLEDGEMENTS

I give thanks to God for bringing me out of horror and giving me the gifts needed to affect change. You save my life every day, and I thank you for the blessings.

Lots of long hours, frustrations, and joys went into creating this book. During its development, I acquired many debts, only a few of which I have space to acknowledge here. First and foremost, I would like to give thanks to my unbelievable Aunt Karen for all of her hard work in helping me write this book. She committed to hours of research, writing, editing, and phone interviews, and she never once complained. I absolutely could not have completed this book without her help.

For constantly encouraging me to be the best that I can, giving me unconditional love and support, and giving me a place that I can call home, I would like to thank my parents, Lori and Randy Ross. Although I came to them later in life, they have loved me as if I was with them since birth and have shown me how parents are supposed to treat their children.

I give thanks to Grandma Paula for transcribing my words and proofreading my manuscript many times, even though it was emotionally draining, and Andrea Nett for providing her editing expertise.

I would also like to give thanks to all of the supports in my life who helped me overcome the traumas of my past, including the entire Ross family, Helen Weiser, Katie Thomas, Susie and Zach

Nettleton, Jack Olsen, Kaylee Beal, Angie Wright, Scott Forrester, Billie Catron, and Josh Niece.

Lastly, I give thanks to the many other people who have influenced my life over the years. It is because of their care and support that I have the courage to continue in the work I do.

DISCLAIMER

When I decided to write this book at such an early age, I knew that it would be limited by my memories, perspective, and experience. It felt a bit presumptuous to try to write an autobiography in my twenties. But my intention was to share my story in hopes that some small bit of good could come out of it, that some small bit of pain could be avoided. The urgency of that desire drove my willingness to risk publishing something that might have come out differently twenty years from now when my life and perspective had matured me further.

The process by which I approached this endeavor was first to document my individual memories and then to match those memories against outside sources to verify the accuracy of my youthful perspective. As I have walked through this process, it has become painfully clear to me how subjective some of my perceptions and memories were. I have realized that time is a very fluid reality in the memory of a child. I now see perspectives, shades, and nuances that did not exist in my childhood experience.

There are individuals that I can remember with exacting detail, and though my childish view of them may be limited, their impact on my life was huge. There are other individuals that I have absolutely no memory of, whatsoever. However, having reviewed my case and counseling records, it is clear that these unknown, unremembered individuals devoted substantial time and effort to my care and recovery. I apologize to those lost faces. I don't know why some were remembered and others were not, but I greatly appreciate everyone who tried to help me to recover, grow, and develop, regardless of the limitations of my personal memories. I truly believe that most of the people I have come in contact with throughout this process have had the best intentions and have only desired my best possible outcome. That said, the truth of the experience my family and I survived is undeniable. My hope is that this book will shed light on the limitations of the existing system that is designed to protect and repair broken families, and the possibilities that may improve how we approach families at risk (in a way that strengthens the life of our communities).

FOUNDATION

The Basis or Groundwork of Anything

I think my earliest complete, conscious memory is my first day of school, when I was three years old. It was a sunny day filled with possibilities, and I was very excited to explore them. I remember thinking, "This is what adults must feel like!" I got on the long yellow bus, which seemed so tall that I thought I would never be able to climb in. With my blue Batman lunch box close to my side for safekeeping, I ascended the stairs to my destiny. I was all set to go, excited to leave home and explore a new world.

Memories, especially childhood memories, are less than complete, and they certainly aren't orderly. As I look back to my first morning of school, I don't remember the fear and pain that became the storyline in later years. I didn't have any bad memories at that point, not really bad memories—not the kind of memories that came later. All I remember are the happy feelings of going to school, coming home and watching television, or playing with Larry, Gary, and Jerry, my younger triplet brothers, and Catina, my older sister.

As I stepped off the bus and walked up the stairs into Faxon Montessori School, I couldn't help but think about how humongous the school was. I was certain at the time that it was big enough to hold a bazillion students. As I walked through the seemingly endless maze of the school, I was filled with joy at the thought of living the life of a "big kid" and thinking about all of the cool friends I would make.

When I finally got to my classroom, the teacher introduced herself and told me to sit in the circle on the carpet with the other students. As I sat there, looking at all the different faces and the varying emotions these faces expressed concerning their first day of school, I noticed that my thoughts were being drowned out by a deafening wail coming from a girl whose dad was dropping off in my class for her first day. She looked as though she had been given a life sentence in a maximum-security prison without the possibility of parole. The sheer horror on her face took my happiness away for a few moments as I started to wonder if this girl was aware of some ominous plight that the rest of us didn't understand. But that fear quickly faded.

After my moment of panic, I started to wonder how this girl could be so terrified at what I perceived to be the best thing that could ever happen to me. I just kept thinking about how lucky I was that I got to be out "on my own" and treated like a big kid, riding the school bus. I was loving school. Little did I know that my love of school would not last forever, nor would the feelings of being excited about the possibilities of the future. I didn't know that soon I would have much more serious concerns.

~

Starved and Scalded, 8-year-old Brothers Die

Missouri Mom Accused of Abusing 2 Triplets

October 24, 1999 | By The Kansas City Star

KANSAS CITY, Mo. — Eight-year-old Larry Bass, who was a triplet, weighed less than 30 pounds when he died Wednesday.

His ribs poked through his sagging skin. His feet, which allegedly had been dunked in scalding water, were badly infected and blood red.

At 2:30 A.M. Friday, Larry's brother, Gary, another triplet, also died. He had been hospitalized with severe burns and malnutrition.

Their mother, Mary Bass, 31, faces multiple assault and abuse charges. More charges could be filed if the deaths are ruled homicides.

"It was the worst case of child neglect I've seen," Police Capt. Darryl Forte said of Larry Bass. "He was just a skeleton covered with skin. He looked mummified. It was like famine you would see in a Third World country.

"He basically died a slow death. It really hurts your heart to see something like that."

Police said the medical examiner's office would wait for the results of some tests before officially declaring the cause of deaths. Charges against Bass could then be upgraded.

In addition to the triplets, Bass had a 12-year-old daughter and a 10-year-old son living with her in a 2 1/2-story house. The third triplet and the two other children have been placed in foster care.[i]

Before the abuse of me and my four siblings started, before the triplets were even born, there was the fighting and abuse between my mother and father. While I don't have a clear memory of what apparently went on between the two of them, there is one night that stands out in my mind.

I remember a night when Ronald Sr., my father, after whom I was named, and Mary, my mother had some friends over for what seemed like a typical social gathering. The evening was fun, with food and conversation, my sister, brothers, and I playing in the midst of the grownup party. After a while, my parents sent us to bed as the party turned more adult, with drinking taking a prominent role. But as kids will, we didn't go right to sleep. From my room, I could hear my mom and dad teasing each other with jokes and things, laughing and having a good time. Then there was a shift, and the teasing became taunting. Taunting quickly turned to trouble as alcohol consumption and tempers increased. I'm not sure who said what to whom, but stabbing words suddenly turned into the sound of someone being slapped across the face. Breaking, pushing, falling, and a rain of hateful words followed. I didn't dare leave my room. Finally, things quieted, and the sounds of the party resumed at a lower level. Eventually, sleep came.

The next morning, my mother was missing two of her teeth. I later found out that my dad had knocked them out while their mutual friends watched the spectacle. Years later, I would learn that this type of thing happened quite often in my house. This, however, was the only instance that I could remember of the two of them fighting that way, and even now I wonder if it was a true memory or one that my mind made up from the stories my mother told us.

I don't have terribly positive memories of, or feelings about, my biological father. I remember him as an abusive man who disappeared from my life when I was quite young. I don't know how much of my impression is from the reality of him, or the lack of him, or the opinions of my mother. Ultimately, she was there, and he wasn't. I believe my father moved to Indiana when he and Mary separated. We saw him sporadically throughout my childhood, then again after the night when we were taken into foster care. He did make some effort at that point, but ultimately, I still see him as the beginning of the problem, rather than the solution.

He hurt us. He hurt my mom. I had to find a way to protect her. Although I was small, I somehow knew this was my job. I had to protect my mom. I had to protect my family.

EXTREMES

Exceeding the Bounds of Moderation

My mother, Mary, was smart, determined, and driven. She could be so much fun, finding ways to entertain us with little or nothing in the way of material things. As I look back at it now, she wasn't much more than a child herself. When she married and had Catina, she would have been about nineteen, twenty-one when I was born, and about twenty-three when the triplets were born. I'm about that age now, and I can't imagine having five children, trying to support them, parent them, and survive, much less make a better life. Many of my best memories of Mary were of her playing with us kids—as one of us. But we lived in a world of extremes, and as suddenly as the good times would start, they would be gone. There would be times when seemingly simple disagreements turned into all-out wars.

Because of the memories I had of my father, I always worried about my mom's boyfriends. I was always on guard, wondering if they were going to snap—wondering what I would do if I were to witness one of them hurting her, debating within myself about how to try and protect her. In addition to my father, Ronald Sr., there was only one other guy, Roosevelt, who brought that fear to reality. Roosevelt was Mary's boyfriend when I was very young, so my memories of him are few. Roosevelt was a tall, heavyset man, and I believe he was Hispanic. Most of the time, he was all right, but his sheer size always made me uncomfortable and frightened. Part of me always knew that a man that big could do some real damage if he wanted to. And he had that kind of quiet menace that you simply feel around some people. With Roosevelt, I always had a sense that there was a line that I'd better not cross, no matter what.

I remember him and my mom fighting only one time. Although I can't think of the actual setting of that day, as I sit here thinking about the event, I picture my siblings and me playing on our porch, laughing and having fun. It was a sunny, bright day, and we were having a great time. We spent a lot of our time playing on the porch when we were little. Since we lived in a bad neighborhood and didn't have a whole lot in the way of material possessions, it was the best we could do, and it was still great fun. We were big on pretend games and could entertain ourselves for hours with make-believe.

As we were playing on the porch, I suddenly heard yelling coming from inside the house. I know I was young, and it may have been the drama of the moment, but at that exact time, I remember the sun hiding itself behind a cloud. I think it was hiding itself from what it knew was about to happen—an image of the blackness of night replacing the day. I remember the rest of that day kind of like a movie. As I saw this change in nature, chills and a cold sweat came over me, and I ran into the house. Just as I entered, I saw Roosevelt, massive and terrifying, launch with all of his force a full jar of hair oil at my mom. It was too late. I was too late. The jar hit her right in the stomach, and she doubled over in pain. I wanted to run to her. I wanted to throw myself in front of her and take on the full weight of Roosevelt's blow. I wanted to treat her as if she were the child, and it was my duty to protect her from all the evils of the world. But I was small. I could barely tie my shoes on my own. I could barely pour my own cereal for breakfast. How was I supposed to help this poor deer caught in the headlights? What could I do to save her from the pain that was hurtling toward her?

I longed at that moment to grow up and be the size of Roosevelt. Then I would show him. Then I would teach him what happens when you mess with the most important thing in my life. I wanted him dead. I wanted to kill him. I wanted to be able to send that jar back, fifty times the speed at which it hit my mom. I wanted the last thing that he saw to be me growing up instantly and crushing his world. But I was just a child. I had no strength outside of my imaginary world. I had no power. I could only watch and be scared.

As the jar hit my mom, and the pain began to work its way through her, I couldn't help but notice the look of genuine shock on her face. Even though she couldn't speak any words, due to the suddenness of the wind being knocked out of her, her face said it all. Her face suggested shock that Roosevelt could even think of doing something like that to her. She looked like a child receiving her first spanking from a parent who had always given her anything she demanded. She looked more hurt by his audacity than from the actual blow.

As she began to cry, my world began to crumble. I couldn't bear seeing her cry. I didn't like having to realize that my mom wasn't invincible, and that there was nothing I could do at the times when she was weak. She turned and ran into the bedroom and locked the door behind her. I didn't mind that she ran and locked herself in her room. I wanted to stand guard at the door and make sure that Roosevelt couldn't break it down to get to her. I wanted to protect her from any more abuse. But Roosevelt didn't try to get to her. He didn't seem all that angry anymore. And the dark clouds that had been hovering in the world of my imagination gave way to the sun again, and life went back to how it was before.

But the feeling of horror that came over my face, over my soul, as I witnessed, for the first time, my mom actually being abused, is still etched in my brain today. I had heard it before, seen the aftermath, but this was the first time I saw it—the first time I truly understood.

PRESSURE

The Exertion of Force upon an Object

Kansas City, MO — Eight-year-old brothers—two of a set of triplets—died after their mother starved them for days and scalded their feet in hot water, authorities say.

Gary Bass, who had been hospitalized with severe burns, died early Friday, police spokesman Sgt. Floyd Mitchell said. His brother Larry, who weighed less than 30 pounds, died Wednesday at their home.

"It was the worst case of child neglect I've seen," homicide Capt. Darryl Forte said of Larry. "He was just a skeleton covered with skin. He looked mummified. It was like famine you would see in a Third World country. He basically died a slow death."

The third triplet was not abused and was placed in foster care, along with two other children who were not abused—a 12-year-old girl and a 10-year-old boy.

Their mother, Mary Bass, called authorities after finding Larry unconscious Wednesday evening. She pleaded innocent Wednesday to assault, abuse and neglect. Other charges could be filed when a coroner's report is received, Jackson County Prosecutor Robert Baird said.

The 31-year-old mother admitted punishing Larry and Gary by putting their feet in scalding water, locking them in a room, and depriving them of food except bread and water for up to two weeks, police said.

The prosecutor had no theory as to why only two of the children were apparently abused.

Bass told police it was hard to work full-time and go back to school while trying to raise the five children, and began withholding food from the two boys this summer when she had trouble controlling them.[ii]

I don't know what happened between Mary and her family of origin. I vaguely remember stories of her being fairly successful in high school, but shortly thereafter, she disappeared and came back pregnant and married. Her parents didn't approve of my biological father, or of her marriage, but they were always good to my siblings and me. Maybe it was because of this, or her youth, or just her competitive, driven personality, but Mary always insisted on well-behaved children. Even in the early days, while there was fun and play, there were also lines you didn't cross with my mother. You didn't show that there were problems in your home. You didn't misbehave in public. You didn't let others "into family business." Family was family, and our family was Mary and the five of us children. No one needed to know what happened here. Those were the rules, and they were not to be broken.

Discipline was always strict, and we were well-behaved children. I remember strangers in the street and Mary's friends in our home always commenting on how well-behaved we were. They were amazed at how well she had raised us. And she was very proud of this. She may have been young and struggling, but she was raising her children right. They minded and did what they were told, and were respectful. Discipline was always a part of our lives, but somewhere along the way, it turned into more than discipline.

I was about six years old when the discipline turned into starvation and severe beatings. It was a gradual change rather than a sudden one, and I remember Mary had a new boyfriend; she always seemed to have a new boyfriend. She seemed more stressed and on edge than usual. From my perspective now, she seemed to be struggling with trying to juggle being a single mother of five and a significant other to a new man she was trying to impress. I know that money was tight because there were times my grandparents or aunts would bring over food or food stamps to help out, but Mary didn't want anyone to know that. She was a very proud woman, and I want to believe that maybe it was her battling with that nature that started some of it. She didn't want anyone to know she was having a hard time, not even us. She didn't want us to think that she couldn't provide for us. So, instead of letting us know that we couldn't afford groceries, she told us that we were not eating because we were bad, and that was our punishment for not listening to her directions. And if we misbehaved, in addition to starving us, what I refer to as "the beatings" began.

I don't know what twisted in Mary; the desire to have well-behaved children turned into the need to have absolute control—to rule with an iron fist, to have us silent and typically out of view, not disturbing her life. While there would be moments of the old Mary, moments of play and caring, they were fewer and further between. And the more rigid the discipline, the abuse, the starvation, the more these glimpses went away.

The desire to survive is strong even in children. During the times when my mom would not feed us, we would have to find ways to get food of some kind. Starving brought out the survival instinct in us, and we had to do whatever was necessary to find nourishment. Mary was a very clever woman. She didn't want anyone to find out that we were being starved during a particular week, so there were times when she wouldn't even allow us to go to school. It also served to further our punishment by making sure that we didn't eat at school. Of course, Mary and whoever her boyfriend was at the time would continue to eat. In fact, toward the end, she became so cruel that she used to make us come downstairs to watch them eat. She would tell us that if we looked away, we were going to get beaten. She would then, of course, play up how well the food tasted by saying things like, "Man, this is some good food. I will definitely need to get seconds, maybe even thirds." Or "I really wish I had children that knew how to be good that I could share this food with, instead of the badass ones I have."

Whenever Mary and her current boyfriend would leave, or go to sleep at night, we would sneak downstairs and dig through the trash cans to see what we could find. Covered with cigarette ashes, coffee grounds, and other filth, we would dig scraps out of the trash. And we wouldn't care. We'd try to wipe off whatever we found in the garbage the best we could, and then we would dig in. We would divide the sometimes rotten and smelly food between the five of us, as much as we could. It did something to us, though, the starving. It made us like the animals you see on the Discovery Channel when there is a drought for a season, and there isn't much to eat. The animals start fighting each other, prepared to kill so that they can survive. Our animal instincts for survival would kick in, and there would be times when there was just enough edible trash for one person, and for a minute or so, we felt prepared to fight to the death over that scrap. Most times, if we couldn't find a way to split the garbage, we would just put it back in the trash so that no one would have it. We would try our hardest to look out for each other like family should, but there were limits, trials that came with desperation.

We would take turns doing favors for each other in exchange for food. It might be anything from getting a crayon to taking a beating. And we'd use those favors, once done, to say that a person owed us food for it. Once, I helped my brother get out of trouble, and when we got to eat later that day, I said to him, "Well, you owe me because of earlier." There was a lot of that going on. "You owe me for..." which meant "I want a little more of your bread" or "I want some more of whatever it is we get to eat later today." Soon that became the normalcy in our life. It was just the way it was for us.

There was a time when we were trying to share food among us right in front of my mom. We were inching the food toward each other very slowly in hopes that, like a T-Rex, she wouldn't see as long as there weren't sudden movements. As we were passing the food around ever so slowly, my mom looked down and saw us. We froze, hoping against hope that she had gone blind and hadn't seen that we were sharing food. She looked at us and gave a smirk that was a cross between "Gotcha!!!!" and "Aw, how cute that you guys are sharing," and then she looked away and continued watching television. I jumped for joy inside my head, silently screaming, "O, thank you, Lord, for not letting us get our food taken away or getting beaten!"

Another time, we were grounded—it wasn't really "grounding" because we never got to do anything anyway. The days of playing on the porch or going places were over by now, but she still called those times "grounding." Mary had gotten KFC and called us downstairs to eat. Now, there is something that you must realize before reading on. At this point, anytime we were called downstairs, it was either to get beaten or to eat. So whenever she would call us, our hearts would start racing a thousand miles an hour. There would be times when we would smell the food from our rooms upstairs, and we would hope and pray that we would get to eat that day. Then we would hear plates being shuffled around, and our hearts would begin to beat faster with excitement as we began to think, "Oh, please, please, please let those plates be for us." Sometimes we would be called down, and other times, we would hear the plates and smell the food but never receive the call. Then we would cry for a bit out of both sadness and frustration.

On this particular day, we did receive the call. However, this was also one of those moments when we couldn't tell what we were going downstairs for. Our mom had previously told us that we weren't going to eat for a week because we did something bad, so we figured that she must have been in the mood to beat us, or that she wanted to torture us by having us watch her and her present boyfriend, Tony, eat. You can imagine our surprise when we got downstairs, and she told us to sit down on the floor because we were about to have dinner. We always sat on the floor like animals when we were able to eat. I think Mary liked towering over us to keep us aware that she was the master and we were the equivalent of lowly servants who could be discarded at any time. But we never minded. We didn't care what she made us do as long as we got fed. So she sat us down on the floor, with our plates and utensils, and filled our plates with food. It was magnificent. My mouth became as salty as if I had been crying as I sat there looking at the beauty of the well-seasoned chicken, the irresistible macaroni and cheese, the exquisite mashed potatoes and gravy, and the ever-scrumptious buttery glory of biscuits. I remember thinking, "This is what Heaven must be like."

As we sat there eating, the television was on, and I remember Mary telling us that we could either get done eating and go to bed, or we could stay up and watch TV. She then went on to add, with the same maniacal smirk that I had seen many times before, "If you want to stay up and watch TV, then you have to receive your beating first." This was at about five o'clock in the evening, so, it was far from bedtime, but most of us didn't want to get beaten just so we could watch a little television. So we tried to eat very slowly in order to soak in as much TV as possible before heading to bed. Of course, my mom caught on quickly and said, "If in two minutes you are still sitting here eating, I am going to assume that you have chosen to receive your beating so that you can stay up." All of us quickly finished eating, thanked her for the food, told her we loved her, and ran upstairs to bed...except for Gary.

Gary was the middle one of the triplets and was always there if you needed a good laugh. He wasn't the brightest of the three, but he was very funny and found humor in even the most desperate of situations. I often thought that he was going to grow up to be a comedian because of his amazing ability to make us laugh even in what seemed like our darkest hour. He had the best heart of anyone I have ever known. His kindness and humor kept me going many times. When Gary was finished eating, he threw his plate away in the trash and sat down in front of the television as if it were his everyday custom. The food almost fell out of my mouth as I watched him sit down. I kept thinking how brave he was but also wondering if he had actually heard and understood what my mom said was going to happen to the ones who stayed up. I kept hoping he would look at me so that I could signal him to run upstairs before it was too late. I had to save him. I couldn't let him take that kind of punishment for a few moments of TV, especially when I wasn't even sure how long my mom would let him stay up after his beating. As I finished eating and went upstairs, I caught his eye and tried to signal for him to follow me. He looked and smiled at me as if to say, "It'll be all right," and he turned back around and continued watching TV. I went upstairs and lay down. When the last of us was done eating and went to bed, I heard the TV go off, and not long after that, Gary's screams started. With each scream of pain that came from his mouth, I winced, praying that she would stop after that one. She beat him for a few minutes, but it felt like hours, and then I only heard Gary crying. After what seemed like an eternity, his crying ceased, and I heard the TV come back on. It was over. Gary survived.

Because I was nowhere near tired, I stayed up in my bed listening to the television and smiling when I would hear Gary laugh. Each of his laughs filled my heart with joy because it told me that he was okay. A few hours later, it was dark, and I heard my mom tell Gary that it was time for bed. He thanked her, said he loved her, and came up the stairs. I ran to his room as I heard him coming up so that I could greet him when he got there. Larry and Jerry were still up, too. Our rooms were small, to begin with, but the triplets' room was so small that they had to share a twin-size bed among the three of them. This forced them to lay sideways on it rather than the traditional way. As I got in their room, Larry and Jerry jumped up, thinking that I might be Mary or Tony coming to beat them. Once they realized it was me, I whispered to them, "Gary is on his way up," and they sat up in their bed as we waited for him.

A few moments later, a small figure limped into the room. As he approached, the moonlight from the window illuminated him, and sorrow filled my body. Every inch of his skin that was visible had defined belt marks on it that were swollen and still bleeding. I was able to see exactly what part of the belt hit him and where. Even though I was used to getting beatings like that, every time I saw those marks, it horrified me as if it were the first time. I wanted to cry for him, but as he limped closer, I realized he was smiling. "What could you possibly be smiling about?" I asked, thinking that the beating must have made him go crazy. He looked at me, beaming, and said, "Mom gave me some gum." He pulled it out of his mouth and showed me. He was such an amazing and uplifting person. Here he was, covered in bleeding bruises, and yet he was filled with joy because he was given a piece of gum.

ALLY

Something United with Another, Especially by Treaty

Man Pleads Guilty in Abuse Case

Mother's Boyfriend Sentenced in Death of Larry, Gary Bass

JOE LAMBE - The Kansas City Star

Jan. 26, 2001 — Tony Dixon watched as his girlfriend, Mary Bass, locked two of her sons in a room and starved them for months. He did nothing again after Bass severely burned the two boys and let them slowly die in pain.

He was stupid and wrong, Dixon said at his guilty plea in Jackson County Circuit Court.

Judge John R. O'Malley sentenced Dixon to a total of 20 years on two counts of child abuse and four of endangering the welfare of a child.

Dixon, 37, admitted that he stood by as Bass abused and ultimately killed the children.

O'Malley questioned Dixon, trying to understand a case the judge said he would never forget.

"How did this happen?"

"She would tell me, `These are my kids. If you don't like the way I raise them, get out.'

"The kids wouldn't let me. Every time they seen me packing my suitcases they would grab my leg and say, `Don't leave us with her.'

"Why didn't you take them to the doctor when you saw them burned?" O'Malley asked.

"Fear mostly, I guess. Call me a coward or whatever. ... It was stupid. I wish I would have did the right thing. I wish I could go back and do it over."

The judge said, "There is an entire metropolitan community that wishes that, too." [iii]

I remember one time when we were so hungry that once Tony had left, we all took turns going downstairs and sneaking peanut butter out of a jar, and eating it. We turned it into a game. We pretended to be secret spies who were after a treasure that had been stolen from them, and we tried to see who could retrieve the treasure the quickest without getting caught. During this time, I was covered with ointment due to an extreme number of bug bites that I had all over my body. For some reason, the bug bites, along with the lack of food, made me sick, and I wasn't able to move around much. When I did move, I itched all over. But I still took my turn going downstairs and getting my taste of the treasure. We thought that we had covered up the fact that we were down there. We figured there was no way Tony could ever figure out that we had gotten into the peanut butter because we put everything back just the way it was. As we sat upstairs laughing, amazed at our cleverness, Tony came upstairs and said, "So which one of you got into the peanut butter?" The smiles vanished from our faces as we realized what he was saying. At first, we tried to deny it, saying, "What peanut butter? We've been up here the whole time." "Bullshit!" Tony said. As I began to realize that we couldn't get away with simply denying it, my survival instincts kicked in, and I shouted, "Gary did it." Before I could stop myself, more came out, "He ran downstairs while you were gone, and he told us that he had gotten some peanut butter." "We told him that we wouldn't tell, but I don't want to get beat for something that I didn't do." Larry, Jerry, and Catina followed cue saying, "Yeah, it was Gary" and "Yeah, Gary did it." To my amazement, Gary looked at us, looked back at Tony, and said, "Yeah, I did it because I was hungry. Sorry."

I wanted to kill myself right then. How could I leave him to be beaten for something that we all partook in? Then Tony said,

"Ronald, what's that on your mouth then?" All of their heads whipped around and looked at me as I quickly wiped my mouth, looked at my hand and said, "It's the ointment from my bug bites." "You're a damn liar," Tony said. Then he continued, "I'm gonna beat yall's asses." Although I was in pure terror at the thought of him beating us, I couldn't help but feel relieved at the same time. I was glad we were all going to get beaten for what we did. I don't know that I'd be able to live with myself today if Tony had believed us and Gary took the beating for us all. I only wish that I had been as brave as he was. I wish that I had the strength to tell Tony that it was just me that had taken the peanut butter, so that the rest of them would have been spared.

He had us line up at the top of the stairs and had us go downstairs one at a time. I don't remember what order it was, but I know that there were at least two of my siblings that went before I had to go. I remember going into Mary and Tony's bedroom. As I walked in, I noticed that the closet had a chair in it and the clothes that normally hung on the rod were laid out across the bed. As he closed the door, he told me to stand on the chair that was in the closet. He then handcuffed me to the rod and began beating me with an extension cord. There was no set amount of times. I was completely at his mercy, unable to shield any part of my body or attempt to run from his blows. As he continued to hit me, I wiggled more and more, knocking over the chair and eventually breaking the handcuffs. That really set him off, and he began to hit me even harder and with even more ferocity.

After we'd all been beaten, we sat together upstairs, tears running down our faces, snot coming out of our noses, unable to put pressure on most parts of our bodies due to the bleeding welts we had, and we began to talk about how much we hated him. We talked about how we wished bad things would happen to him that would make him feel the pain that he had caused us. The longer we sat talking about the things we wished to happen, the more we would start to laugh. We first wanted him to get hit by a car, and then we decided a train would be better, and then falling out off a plane pissing himself all the way down became the best option. We were just trying to think of things that would make us laugh. We wanted to think of anything else but the welts and immense pain we were in.

~

We quickly learned that Tony's mood swings could be comparable to Mary's at times. One day, I was sitting downstairs and talking with Tony and my mom, and something came up about my father, Ronald Sr. As the conversation went on, I made a joke about how Tony wasn't my dad. We all laughed it off, and I thought nothing of it, until it came time to eat the next day and Tony told me that I wasn't able to eat for a week, though he made sure that everyone else was able to, and I would just have to watch. Later, when I heard Tony was gone, I went downstairs and asked my mom why Tony was punishing me. She said, "Well, Junior, you really hurt Tony's feelings when you said he wasn't your dad." She continued, "He works really hard for you kids, and your ungrateful attitude really pissed him off." She then told me that if I apologized to him when he came home, she would allow me to eat again.

~

Being called downstairs caused a panic, but after a while, being called downstairs happened less often as we were confined to our bedrooms on the second floor of our mostly empty house. At that time, the trigger for the panic would be adult feet on the stairs. When we would hear Tony or Mary coming up the stairs, we didn't know if they were coming upstairs to beat us or to give us food. And if they were giving us food, we were always worried that one of us might be told that we couldn't eat. Sometimes they would come upstairs and have a plate of ten or so sandwiches, and they would say things like, "You can't eat today, Ronald" or "Since you were bad yesterday, you can't eat today, Jerry." The person that was unable to eat that particular meal would just have to sit there and watch the others eat. Sometimes we were nice enough to try to share and sneak food to each other, even though we weren't supposed to. There were lots of times, however, when we were just as hungry as the person who wasn't able to eat, and we would take advantage of having that extra bit of food because we didn't know when we'd be able to eat next. I hate how subhuman we became because of them. I'm still shocked and surprised that people could be so evil as to make children fight with each other over bits of food like ravenous dogs.

Once, the starvation got so bad that I got my hands on an empty little Chinese food container and filled it up with sugar. I would take a spoon and just eat straight sugar. As I closed my eyes and ate spoonful after spoonful of pure sugar, I would pretend that I had won a trip to an all-you-can-eat buffet at some Chinese food place, and I'd pretend that I got a plate and put a mountain-high heap of rice on it. For a couple of weeks, that was about all I would eat.

Our perception of time began to suffer during the worst of it. There were lots of times when all of us would sleep throughout the day, because we didn't have the energy to do anything else. We were very weak, very malnourished. In the summertime, it got really hot in our house—there was no air-conditioning, at least not in our rooms, and Kansas City summers are hot and muggy. When we would get thirsty, Mary would tell us, "Too damn bad!" or "Maybe if you weren't bad children, I would allow you to get some water."

At night, we would wait until Mary and Tony were silent long enough to assume they were asleep. Then we would sneak to the bathroom and get water from the faucet without being too loud, because if they heard the faucet running, Mary or Tony would soon come upstairs to beat us. As the water would hit my tongue, it would taste so sweet. My mouth was so dry, and my body so deprived of anything nourishing that the water tasted as though I were biting into a juicy fruit. I would imagine that I had bought a smoothie with lots of chopped fruit in it. It was so delicious, and I would fill up on as much water as I could. However, later on, that water would make me sick, and I would vomit it all back up. Then I would be so weak that I would stumble back to bed and fall asleep, hoping that I would die and not have to wake up to the pain and hunger again.

~

I was not a big fan of Tony and his abusive tendencies. However, my mom seemed to really enjoy his company as much as he enjoyed hers, and he also enjoyed the free room and board that came along with it. Although Tony was respectful of my mom most of the time, there was one night that I can clearly remember Tony and Mary getting into a fight. They were yelling at each other, and Tony started to walk upstairs to get away from her, opting for distance instead of physical violence. But Mary kept egging him on, kept trying to set him off. As he was walking away, up the stairs, she hit the mark. I don't know what she said, but he came rushing back down the stairs and grabbed her with his hands around her throat. He was screaming in her face, with his hands around her throat, looking as if he was going to choke her. But she wouldn't back down; she was screaming right back in his face. She was yelling, "Just do it." My mom was a fighter; that's one of the things you have to understand. She was never passive. It was not like she would just take a beating, or take being yelled at. She would fight back; she would stand her ground. Tony kept his hands around her throat, and they continued screaming at each other, but he didn't hit her. I remember that I was sitting next to her on the couch while this scene played out.

All I wanted, at that moment, was to have a big, heavy bat in my hand. If I had had a bat, I could have just knocked him out. I would've shown him. He couldn't treat my mom like that. She was my mom, and I would do anything for her. I felt so helpless and cowardly. I hated that feeling. There was nothing I could do, and that frustrated me, enraged me. All I wanted to do was to protect her.

It doesn't make any sense from a logical perspective since we were getting beaten by her as well as him, and were starved by her as well as him, but she was my mom. She was my world. He was the evil one, and she had to be protected from him, and I couldn't do it. I can't tell you how powerful that feeling of helplessness was—and still is, in some ways.

CALM

Without Rough Motion

I guess one of the hardest things to explain is that, until the end, things weren't all good or bad. The good and bad mixed together and formed a strange "normal" that was all we knew of life. Sometimes we went to school; sometimes we didn't. Sometimes we were allowed out of the house; sometimes we weren't. It was our world. It made sense to us, as much as anything could. But it wasn't predictable. Maybe that was the most consistent part—the lack of consistency.

We had two golden retrievers growing up: Trish and Bandon. They were unlucky as well, and were just as hungry as we were. I remember we used to have them chase us around the house, because we were bored outside. Sometimes we didn't have any strength, because we hadn't eaten for a few days, but we would try to muster up some kind of energy to go and play, and it would be great. We'd run around the entire house, and when we got to the deck, Trish and Bandon would stop chasing us. Then they'd run around the house and wait for us to come and chase after them.

One of our favorite weekend outings was piling into Mary's boyfriend's car, whomever she was seeing at that time, and going dumpster diving. We'd drive to where she thought the best stuff would be, to rich neighborhoods, or where the good stuff was likely to be tossed out, and we'd go digging through them. It sounds kind of gross now, but it was one of my favorite things to do. And people really do throw away good stuff sometimes.

While generally we played alone and were fairly isolated, I do remember neighbors. I also remember extended family, babysitters, and daycare. I remember trips to parks, picnics, outings; at least before the very end, then the walls kind of pulled in on us. But before things got too bad, on nice days, we could go outside. We could play in the yard. We could play on the porch, and even go to the park.

There was a little white girl who lived in the house right next to us, and she would sometimes come out to play. I don't remember her name, but I believe she was homeschooled, because she was around during the days when we weren't going to school regularly. We weren't allowed to leave the yard, and neither was she, but I remember my siblings and I would talk to her from our mutual gate. We built these complex fantasy games in which we would pretend we were going on these great adventures and quests. We'd pretend that her side was some kind of fortress and our side was some kind of fortress. We would have a lot of fun playing together without ever crossing those fortresses' lines. When we were playing, we got lost in the games. We didn't worry about time or what would happen inside later. We were all just kids playing.

When we got taken away after my brothers died, I was worried about the dogs. I remember that we were told that the little girl's family took them. I don't know what happened to them after that, but it was a comfort knowing that they were going to someone we at least knew and liked.

Some of the "good times" came from my mom's obvious poor judgment. There was one particular time when I was seven or eight years old, and my mom was drinking a Colt 45. For those who don't know, Colt 45s are tall cans of cheap beer. I remember asking her for some, because I was a little kid and saw my mom drinking something, so I wanted some, too. Now, a normal parent would say "Hell, no," or "You're not old enough," but my mom decided instead to give me a can of my own. So there I was at seven or eight years old drinking this whole can of Colt 45 and getting drunk for the very first time with my mom. I had the worst headache of my entire life and was totally nauseated. I didn't vomit, though I probably would have been less miserable if I had. But I thought I was pretty special when she handed me that can. I remember my mom laughing and giving me some medication to help me sleep. That was my first time being drunk because of Mary, but it was not my last. There were times when she would buy wine coolers and Boone's Farm and would let Catina and me drink some of whatever she was having. I remember the wine coolers and Boone's Farm tasting like soda, and I kept asking her for more. It was like we were some of her friends when she let us drink with her. Like we were grownups.

~

For a time, Mary went to community college while continuing to work full-time. When she finally graduated, we all went to her graduation. Afterwards, we went to the local donut shop, got donuts, and went home. We didn't have any power in our house, so we lit candles and ate donuts in the living room and just talked for hours. All of us: Larry, Gary, Jerry, Catina and myself along with Mary and Tony. We were all sitting there. It was a happy time.

There were times when we'd go to the park and would try to have a picnic. There were times when we'd be a normal family, or at least try to be as normal a family as was possible for us. And we were a family for the most part. Things have fractured now, but then, we were fiercely united as a family.

Once when the triplets, Catina, and I were at the park without our mom, these other kids from the neighborhood started trying to pick on us. They were trying to hit us with sticks and rocks. We all banded together at the top of the jungle gym and launched a defensive strike. We worked together as a team and started throwing rocks back at the kids, pelting them wherever we could. After a few direct hits, the kids eventually stopped and ran off. We began cheering and hugging each other atop the jungle gym. We had won a skirmish, a little war, as a family, and it was a great feeling. We really felt that together, as a family, no one could break us. Our confidence was firmly grounded in being a family, being together.

Even though our family had some truly horrific issues, it wasn't like every day was a fight for our lives, per se. Until the end, it wasn't as though we were getting beaten every day, all day. I know that doesn't make any of the awful things better, but it does kind of explain the conflicted feelings I have about each of my siblings and about our mother. There was good in the bad, and bad in the good.

HOPE

The Feeling That What Is Wanted Can Be Had or That Events Will Turn Out for the Best

A. Factual Summary[iv]

In March 1995, DFS received the first of many hotline calls alleging Bass was battering and starving her five children, Ronald, Catina, and triplets, Larry, Gary, and Jerry. DFS investigated various abuse and neglect reports and visited the Bass home; however, DFS never deemed the hotline reports warranted local law enforcement notification or removal of the children from the home. On August 16, 1999, DFS received a hotline call in Jefferson City, Missouri. The caller reported: (1) scratches were seen on Larry's chest; (2) Bass was starving her children as punishment; (3) Bass had locked Ronald in the basement; (4) the children were searching through trash cans for food; (5) all five children appeared dehydrated and malnourished with sunken eyes and protruding ribs; and (6) the children were so weak they could not drink from a glass without assistance. The hotline information was faxed immediately to Kansas City, Missouri, where a DFS employee screened the information according to MDSS protocol and determined a family assessment and services approach, (1) rather than an investigation, (2) was warranted.

Johnson was assigned to perform a family assessment that day on the Bass family. Johnson went to the Bass home, where she met Bass's live-in boyfriend, Tony Dixon, at the front gate. Dixon told Johnson Bass was working and the children were not at home. Johnson told Dixon to have Bass call her. The following day, Bass called Johnson at work, and Johnson returned to the Bass home to perform a family assessment. During her visit, Johnson talked to Bass, and interviewed three of the children, Ronald, Catina, and Jerry. Johnson did not see or interview Larry and Gary. Bass told Johnson that due to their behavioral problems, Larry and Gary lived with their natural father. The children also told Johnson that Larry and Gary were living with their father. Dixon, however, told Johnson that Larry and Gary were out of town visiting their grandparents. Johnson recognized the discrepancy and recorded Dixon's seemingly contradictory statement on the family assessment form. Johnson also noted Bass "was to contact [Johnson] if Larry and Gary returned home." At no time did Johnson verify Larry's and Gary's whereabouts.

Johnson spent an hour in the Bass home. She confined her visit to the living room, which she observed to be very clean. Johnson smelled food cooking on the kitchen stove. Bass denied ever punishing her children by locking them in the basement or by withholding food from them. The children told Johnson that Bass took good care of them. The children denied Bass withheld food, locked them in the basement, or otherwise abused them. Bass attested that Johnson assured Bass she would follow-up with another visit in two weeks. The family assessment form does not indicate any intention to follow-up, nor did Johnson follow up with the family.

Following her home visit, Johnson determined no social services were needed, and she concluded the Bass children were safe, despite never seeing Larry and Gary. Johnson turned in her family assessment report without completing a mandatory safety assessment. By a form letter dated September 7, 1999, Johnson informed Bass DFS was not opening a case "because we agreed during our discussion that your family is not in need of services." Two weeks later, Johnson's supervisor, Rosa, reviewed the report and completed the safety assessment, thereby certifying the Bass home was safe, without ever being in the Bass home or seeing the Bass children.

~

I don't know if Mary tried to get help when we were growing up. I remember her saying she went to get assistance, and they told her she didn't need help. We sometimes had food stamps and that sort of thing; occasionally, we even went to a daycare center. But I don't remember any kind of comprehensive effort to help our family. Mary's parents, our grandparents, and her sisters would bring over food or food stamps, but money was always tight.

I remember a couple of different instances when social workers came to check our family—particularly one that came toward the beginning of the beatings and starvation. The social worker seemed pretty nondescript to me. She came into the living room, and asked us questions about how we were treated by Mary. Mary was sitting there with us in the living room when the questions were asked. The social worker stayed for an hour or so, and we acted as if we were normal kids in a normal family. Mary knew they were coming; we had been warned.

We tried to act as normal kids do around people who aren't their parents. We tried to "test the water" and see if maybe we could get away with a bit more, because we knew Mary wasn't going to do anything in front of company. Of course, it turned out to be a big mistake in the end, but at the time we were talking, because we were being starved at that point, we'd say things such as, "Well, can we eat now?" Or, "Mom, when are we going to eat?" Or, "Can we have this and this and this for dinner?" We were pretending as if it were something that we always got to do. And she would just give us looks that said, "You just wait until this woman leaves," and we knew we were going to be in huge trouble, but we just had to do it. We figured that maybe she would have to feed us while the lady was there to prove that we weren't being starved. But I remember the lady never had to have any proof of any kind that we were all right. She didn't ask to see the house, or to see us eat, or even to see our rooms. It was just word of mouth, mostly Mary's words, and that was good enough for her.

They did separate us to ask us questions, but Mary was always in the room. Even if Mary wasn't in the room, I think we still wouldn't have said anything bad about her. I wouldn't have. I didn't want to risk the chance that we would get taken from Mary. She was our mother, our family. We were a team. And what if we were taken away but ended up back with her again? What would happen then? How much worse would it be then? Especially if we were the cause of my mom's embarrassment. If it was our fault. If it was my fault.

Today, my biggest question is why anyone who suspected abuse was taking place would ask a child about it with the suspected abuser sitting in the same room, glaring down at the child, fully able to hear and retaliate. I'm not sure anything we said would have made a difference; we were pretty conditioned by then. But I do wonder if maybe something would have slipped if they had asked us alone, or looked around the house, or something other than believing Mary's lies. Our lies. I wonder if my brothers would still be alive. If I could have been a bit braver and spoken up, could I have saved them, or would it have fallen on deaf ears? It was very clear to me that the social worker wasn't interested in what was really happening; she was just filling out her forms and moving on.

After the social worker left, all hell broke loose, and we were starved for another couple weeks, with occasional bread and water to keep us alive, along with the beating we got right afterwards. Mary was really angry about the "food" comments when the social worker was there. But it was worth it to us, for a chance that maybe we would get to eat. We had to try. It was something to hope for.

~

Food was our focus. Our goal. Our only desire. At that point, we'd wake up every morning, and that would be the thing that we hoped for. We didn't hope that we would get to watch cartoons or that we would get toys or something like that. It was, "I hope that I get to eat today." "I hope that we get food today." "I hope that we get fed more than once," which was a rare occurrence, but that was like our Christmas. And we never knew. Every day was different. There wasn't any real predictability to it. We just didn't know if we were going to get food or not, and it was like a gift if we received a sandwich. It was a gift if we got half a bowl of salad, or if we got the leftovers of whatever Mary and Tony had the night before. Scraps were wondrous.

Although we children took the biggest hit in the lack-of-food department, there were times when Mary and Tony also felt the sting of being poor. I remember a time when we were so poor that we had to make pancakes out of flour and water. There was nothing else in them. No baking powder, butter, or eggs. And the syrup was made from sugar that had been boiled in water. We were so hungry that even though the pancakes tasted awful, we stuffed our faces and pretended we had gone out for a fancy meal. We just drenched the flour cakes in sugar water and took full advantage of the fact that we were finally able to eat something.

FEAR

A Distressing Emotion Aroused by Impending Danger, Evil, Pain, etc.

There was one night where we were all sharing a room—Catina, Jerry, Larry, Gary, and I. We didn't have frames for our beds, so the mattresses were right on the floor. It was summer in Kansas City, so was very hot and muggy. The windows were open, and we had a box fan on the floor. We decided to hook our covers into the fan, turned the fan on high, and blew the covers up so that they turned into a roof for our bed tent. We all slept in the tent that night, camping in our room.

In the middle of the night, my mom came running up the stairs and burst into our room. The tent went flying. She was in a panic. Someone had tried to break into the house, and she scared him away with a butcher knife from the kitchen.

Rather than being scared, my adrenaline kicked in, and I went into fight mode. After my mom told us that she was going back downstairs to check on everything and to see what Tony was up to, I rallied the rest of my siblings together, and we began fortifying our room in case the man decided to come in through our window. We started pushing things against the window and putting sharp things all around it. We covered the floor with dangerous things so that anyone stepping into the room would really hurt themselves, fall out the window, or allow me time to get the metal bat my mom had left with me so that I could beat him to death. We were all awake for the next few hours, sitting together in the room, hoping that whoever it was didn't try to come back. I stayed up until morning started to lighten the sky, to make sure that we were safe.

Tony was downstairs during the robbery attempt. Nothing was taken. The would-be robber didn't even make it inside the house because Mary had scared him away. The next day, my grandpa came over with a gun and gave it to my mom to keep in the house, just so there was more protection for her if something like that ever happened again. I don't know if she actually kept it or not, but I have no memory of ever seeing it after that night.

Although we were scared at the possibility that the burglar might want to kill us, it felt like it was a danger we could do something about. We could fight the burglar. And a sense of empowerment filled my spirit, even if temporarily.

~

My mom was the kind of person who always needed to have a man in her life. She didn't like being alone. In the beginning, Catina's and my biological father, Ronald Sr., filled that need, then the triplets' biological father. As you may have noticed earlier, the triplets and I are really close in age—18 months apart, in fact. Mary got pregnant by their father during the period my dad was out of the picture. Eventually, my mom split from their dad and got back together with Ron Sr., but it was short-lived, and he eventually left the family permanently. Then there were several other boyfriends before she ended up with Tony. She was always trying to find or keep a boyfriend. Even though she had five children who loved her, if she didn't have a man in her life, she considered herself alone.

Unfortunately, the best times that we had with my mom were the times when she was single. When there wasn't a man around, Mary acted like an actual mom and tried to take care of us as best she could. Money was always tight, and she was constantly stressed, but when she wasn't trying to keep a man in her life, she was focused on us. Of course, that would change as soon as she would find another interest, or an old one would come back.

By the time she was with Tony, even her attitude toward us when she was alone changed. I remember a time when she and Tony broke up after one of their many bad fights. As a result of their fight, Tony moved out of the house, leaving Mary "alone." When we tried to comfort our depressed mother, she screamed at us, telling us that it was our fault that he left. She screamed, "If I didn't have so many bad children, he might have stayed." And then she began beating us. She really meant it. She blamed us for his leaving. She didn't talk to us for a couple of weeks, except when she absolutely had to, because she thought that we drove him away.

Tony eventually came back to my mom, and things were okay in her world again, at least for a while. Then months later, they would get into another argument, and Tony would "move out" of the house, leaving my mother to take her frustrations out on us. One of the times that Tony and Mary broke up, she had dropped us off at daycare and told us that if he tried to come and pick us up, not to go with him. This was one of the few times she had initiated a breakup, and she let us know that she didn't want him in her life anymore. We acknowledged what she told us and had every intention of not going with him if he showed up. But that afternoon, he came to pick us up, and the daycare people told us to go with him. I wanted to tell the staff what my mom had told us, but I couldn't muster the courage to do so. I kept thinking about all the times she blamed us for men leaving, and I didn't want to be the cause of them not getting back together if that's what she decided to do. I wanted to tell him no so badly. I wanted to have the old Mary back. But I couldn't say anything. I felt so helpless. So useless. If I couldn't protect my family in this moment, how was I supposed to take charge when things were really bad? I didn't want to disappoint my mom by disobeying, but we were also raised to mind those in charge of us. And we couldn't refuse to go with Tony, because we feared that he would beat us if we did, and we didn't want to get ourselves in more trouble. As it turned out, my initial fear was correct, and Mary and Tony got back together again after he picked us up. So, in the end, I guess it turned out well, at least for them, and at least for the moment.

RACE

A Group of Persons Related by Common Descent or Heredity

I don't remember my mom telling me why she hated Larry and Gary, and even Jerry at times, but while we were all subject to her rages, there was definitely a difference.

My assumption was that her rage had a lot to do with the fact that they were half white. That was the only significant difference that constantly stood out. They weren't any better or worse than Catina or me. They were smaller, but nothing else made sense in my head. I know that Catina was fierce in her desire to remain with a black family when we were finally separated. When that didn't happen, she found her own. So while it wasn't that clearly explained, my perception was that Mary hated the white part of the triplets, even though she dated and got pregnant by a white guy. That was part of the reason why she beat them and part of the reason why I felt she took better care of my sister and me. Once, while she was downstairs beating Larry, Jerry, and Gary, Catina and I were upstairs with Tony, and he said, "Maybe she wouldn't be so crazy if she had just stopped with you two." I took that as a reference to our racial makeup as well as the increased challenges of five children as opposed to two.

We grew up in predominantly black neighborhoods, but Mary periodically worked with and had friends who were Hispanic and white. Roosevelt was Hispanic; at least, that's how I remember him. I don't remember the triplets' father, but clearly, Mary had chosen to date and have sex with a white man and have his children when she became pregnant.

I remember Mary talking about how much harder people were on her because she was black and how unfair things were for black people in general. But I don't remember her directing prejudice specifically outwardly toward white people. It wasn't as if she hated white people openly and vehemently. She just hated the white that was in her three boys.

I've always ended up in relationships with people who were white. I don't think it's because I have a real preference one way or another. I lived in predominately white cities during the beginning of my dating years, so I've always just been in situations where the person I've fallen for happened to be white. But I do know, when I think about having kids one day, I've always seen them as biracial— something that I think has more to do with my lost brothers than it does with dating preference.

It wasn't until just recently when my adopted mom, Lori, was talking to me and asked me about the racial tension my mom felt and her feelings of dislike toward whites that I started to think that maybe that's why I have a strong inclination to want biracial children. I had never really thought about it, but maybe, subconsciously, I feel that if I have biracial children, I will treat them better than Mary treated my brothers, and that will make things better. I wonder if my feelings of guilt and sadness about losing my two biracial brothers have anything to do with that. It's an interesting thought, and I suspect there's something to it. But I guess I'll have to figure it out for myself as my life progresses.

COMMUNITY

A Social, Religious, Occupational or Other Group Sharing Common Characteristics or Interest

Triplets' Mom Guilty in Deaths of Two Sons
Posted: Sunday, October 22, 2000
By The Associated Press
KANSAS CITY, Mo. — A woman who said her multiple personalities were responsible for the deaths of her two 8-year-old triplet sons was convicted of two counts of second-degree murder Saturday.

Mary Bass, 32, had pleaded not guilty by reason of insanity. Her lawyers and defense experts said she had severe psychosis and a personality named "Sharon" who controlled her actions.

Police said Bass locked Gary and Larry Bass in a room and deprived them of food and dipped their feet in scalding water as punishment. The boys died in October 1999.

Bass's other triplet, and two other children are in foster care.

Besides murder, she was convicted of 10 other charges, including various child abuse charges. Jurors recommended eight life sentences, plus 32 years in prison. She was acquitted on a 13th charge of child abuse.

After the verdict was read, Bass leaned over and whispered to her defense counsel. Later, after one of her lawyers headed to the bench, Bass was seen smiling and appeared to be laughing softly.

At trial, Bass was erratic. At one point, a prosecutor asked a defense expert about "Sharon," described as a cruel alternate personality.

Bass yelled, "Well, what you don't understand? Gee!" and was quieted by her lawyer. She then tore at her hand with a pen, which was taken away, and then used her fingers to scratch her wrist until she bled.

On Friday, she was removed from the courtroom after she cursed a prosecutor and yelled, "No, no, no, no — I'd rather kill myself than kill my kids." She later laughed to herself as a prosecutor asked jurors to send her to prison.

Psychologist Marilyn Anne Hutchinson said Bass developed multiple personalities to cope with sexual and physical abuse as a child. Prosecutors agreed Bass had mental problems but rejected the multiple-personality diagnosis and insisted she knew right from wrong.

Bass' boyfriend, Tony Dixon, 37, is also charged with child abuse and endangering a child in the case. His court date hasn't been set.

Medical experts called the case one of the worst they had seen.

When police arrived at the Bass home after a 911 call from one of the Bass children, Larry was found dead of malnutrition. Gary was found upstairs lying on a filthy mattress, emaciated and so badly infected that his burned toes and part of his empty stomach had gangrene; he died two days later.

Records recently made public showed social workers thought the children had been abused repeatedly, but didn't recommend removing them before the two boys died. Officials at Missouri's Division of Family Services said the state has since changed its procedures.

My mom never went to church with us. We never were a family that went to church. However, she did send us to a babysitter who went to church. And she let that babysitter take us to her church whenever she went. I remember that I didn't know the rules of church. I didn't know how a church service was supposed to go or what behavior was appropriate or inappropriate. At one of the church services, Jerry and I got so bored that we started playing around in the pews, pretending we were off in some other land, having an adventure. The babysitter who took us to church was not happy with our clear disregard for the Lord and proper worship and began pinching and hitting our legs while telling us to straighten up and act right. I remember getting really mad at her because she wasn't our mom and had no right to discipline us in any manner. My defiant side came out in that moment, and I refused to let her see me react to the pain. I would not give her the satisfaction of seeing me cry or acknowledge in any way that I was in the wrong. But, it was interesting because that's my only memory of any kind of church activity. That was my only memory of any formal relationship to God—an absence of understanding or caring, and boredom with listening about a spiritual figure that had never revealed his existence in the life I was living then.

Besides unpleasant church experience, I remember my mom telling me that children didn't go to hell, but adults did. She told me kids who were old enough to believe in Jesus Christ and in God could go to hell, because they were able to distinguish between right and wrong, and they could tell if what they were doing was okay or not.

I wonder, now, how she justified her behavior. But what she said did stick with me. I do believe deeply in Jesus Christ. I believe that children are innocent and can't be condemned to hell, but that's mostly because I don't believe in the concept of hell. Looking back on it, I think it's kind of funny that she tried to teach us this when our home life was the way it was, which was definitely not Christian.

~

We saw Mary's parents fairly often. In fact, there were times when they would babysit all five of us while Mary went to work. After one of the times when an investigator had come to our house to see if the allegations of child abuse were true, I remember my mom being very angry at my grandma. After overhearing a conversation, I found out that her anger stemmed from a belief that my grandma was the one who called the hotline on her. So for a while, we were not able to see any of my extended family. Mary was mad at them and was willing to cut them out of her life completely for betraying her. After all, they broke of the sacred rules of our culture and family: don't talk to outsiders about family business. Thankfully, Mary got over her anger at my grandparents, and visits eventually resumed. As I think about it now, I'm sure her desperation for a babysitter that would not charge her a fee heavily influenced her ability to get over her hurt feelings.

I also believe that it was my grandma that called the hotline on my mother, and I can recall instances where she disobeyed directions my mother had given her about our care. I remember a time when Mary dropped us off at our grandparent's house and told our grandparents not to feed us. She said we had already eaten and didn't need to eat while we were there since it was going to be a short visit. As soon as she left, my grandma asked us if we were hungry and everyone said yes without hesitation. She said, "I thought so," and went to get us some food. Grandma even went as far as feeding us several times over the few hours we were there to make sure our bellies were plenty full before we went back home. My grandma was always so nice to us, and loving. My grandpa was, too, though he wasn't a direct caregiver for us. They were good people, and I miss having a relationship with them.

My mom had several siblings and would occasionally drop us off with them while she worked or ran errands. There was one time when my mom dropped us off with my aunt Jean, at my grandparents' house. It was always strange to me that Jean lived with my grandparents, even though she was an adult with a kid of her own. I could never figure out what was wrong with her, but remember my mom saying that she had some kind of instability. It is interesting to me that she would classify my aunt in this way, as it would eventually be her chief defense in the deaths of my brothers. Anyway, we were dropped off with Jean one night and had a sleepover at my grandparents' house. The night was pretty standard for us. We watched television and had a snack before settling in on the floor in the living room for the night. Well, the next morning, we weren't supposed to turn on the TV, but being children, decided we would anyway, as long as we turned the volume down quickly before our aunt heard anything. Well, we didn't get it down fast enough, because it was loud, and it woke Jean up. I remember her coming into the living room with a switch from one of the trees outside and spanking our butts. When our mom came to pick us up later in the day, I told her that I hated Jean and explained what she had done to us, looking to my mom in hopes that she would avenge our spanking. She didn't. We got spanked because we did something wrong, and Mary made sure I understood that.

I am sure, in their day, my grandparents were strict, but they were never abusive toward us kids. My aunt Jean and my aunt Janet seemed very comfortable with their parents. They were a family. Each of my Aunts had kids of her own, and the kids seemed to do well. When we were around, they treated us like family. It always felt safe with them. I suspect something may have happened to Mary when she left home, then came back, married and pregnant at such a young age, but she never spoke about that time, so I am left only with stories from my grandparents and my own speculation. I don't have the sense that she was with my biological father the whole time she was away. But that was in her late teens.

~

I understand that in her trial, Mary tried to use a defense of multiple personalities based on sexual and physical abuse from her childhood, which caused an alternative personality named "Sharon" to take over and cause her to do terrible things. Whatever abuse Mary was talking about, I don't think that it stemmed from her childhood with my grandparents. I never experienced any hint of abuse with them. Nor did I hear her talk about significant negative family events during her childhood. Mary hated it when her family would "get in her business" or tell her how to raise us. She would cut off all contact when they didn't treat her with "respect," or would argue with her about our condition, or when she felt they had betrayed her. But I never saw any lingering evidence of abuse or fear of abuse from her parents. If anything, she could be highly aggressive toward them when confronted; she certainly wasn't timid.

Mary's mood could switch in a minute with very little cause. We never quite knew if she would be angry, happy, tired, or bored—though, all were emotions that could lead to beatings. She had weird episodes, more like a manic phase or a rage phase. Clearly, she had extreme reactions. But I never met "Sharon." There were no changes in Mary's voice, demeanor, word choices, posture, or behaviors before she beat or starved us. She never indicated that she had lost time or didn't remember what she had done or why. She remembered everything. She always said we deserved it.

I never saw any evidence of what I, as an adult, now know would indicate multiple personality disorder or any other dissociative disorder. I believe that Mary was very stressed out from trying to survive and raise five children by herself. I believe that Mary didn't have the maturity required to manage her complex life (low income, survival stresses, work, school, multiple difficult relationships, and five children). I believe that she did not seek, did not receive, and, in fact, rejected the community support she needed to make good choices and live them out. But it was Mary who loved us, played with us, beat us, starved us, and killed my brothers. Well, it was Mary and Tony.

There was no one named Sharon in our house. In my opinion, the rest of that was just a desperate attempt to try and minimize repercussions after everything had been discovered.

VACATION

A Period of Suspension of Work, Study or Other Activity, Usually Used for Rest, Recreation, or Travel

One night, or early morning I guess, we left the duplex we were living in and piled into Tony's car for what was one of our first and only vacations ever. It was probably around 4 o'clock in the morning, and we were told to be very quiet in order to make sure no one knew we were leaving. Mary didn't want our neighbors to know because we lived in a pretty rough neighborhood, and Mary knew that if the rest of the neighbors knew we were gone, it would increase our chances of getting robbed.

So, we left in the early hours, before it was light, and headed to Louisiana. Tony's mom lived in Louisiana, and Mary wanted to go meet her. We were going on a road trip, a vacation. Even saying it now makes me feel like something I dreamed up.

But it was real, and it was so fun. I remember how happy our drive was all the way there. We listened to Michael Jackson and other artists from that era on the way there, which included some Janet and Toni Braxton. It was one of the happiest times of my life with Mary, and, though it pains me to say it, with Tony. I loved oldies music because it was a connection that everyone in my family had to each other—a sort of glue that attempted to keep us together.

We stopped at a Jack-in-the-Box on our way there, and I remember it pretty well because it was the first time I had ever eaten there, and it was always a big treat when we got to eat out. One of the other reasons this particular eating establishment stands out in my memory so well is because it was close to Halloween, and I remember that they put us kids' meals into these Halloween buckets that glowed in the dark. It was the best thing ever. I not only got to eat at Jack-in-the-Box, but I got to keep this souvenir from the best trip we'd ever taken as a family. I don't remember much about being in Louisiana—or even if it was Louisiana, to be honest. I just remember red sand and red clay dirt. I also remember going fishing with Tony. It was almost like a father-son experience, and it was the closest thing I ever had to one, up until the time I went into foster care. He showed me how to bait a line and the proper way to cast it out. It was one of the only times that I ever felt that I had a dad— that I had someone who cared about me and wanted to teach me all of the things he knew, so that I could pass it on to my son one day. Best of all, we got to eat three meals a day, plus snacks, while we were down there, and no one received a beating. It truly was the best family week that I ever experienced with Mary and Tony.

~

While most kids looked forward to and loved summer break, I often dreaded that time of year and became saddened at the idea of being stuck in my room all summer. I remember at times being really depressed because, during the summer months, Catina would go off to D.A.R.E camp during the day, and since I didn't have a TV or toys, I just had to sit in my room all day alone. Larry, Gary, and Jerry were unable to play because they had to stay in their own room for something they did or didn't do. Sometimes it was just because Mary and/or Tony didn't feel like letting them play. So I was just stuck by myself, sitting on my floor doing absolutely nothing. I had a couple of books in my room, and often became so bored that I would try to teach myself to read. But since I didn't have a clue how to read, I would make up my own stories. The stories that I created in the books I read allowed me to live out my fantasies about how I wished my life was. When I wasn't living out my ideal life in books, I would walk around my bedroom pretending that I was on different types of adventures. Most times I would go to places that had lots of food. There were times when I would just walk around the corners of my room, and try to play out songs in my made-up version of sign language, or I would just think up songs to sing because I didn't have anything else to do. I spent a lot of time in make-believe places during those long summer months.

When Catina came home in the afternoons, I was always so excited because I would have someone to play with. We would play games like *Mother May I?* and there was a game where we would name different kinds of pies. I don't remember the specifics of the game, but it was almost like Red *Light, Green Light*, where you would name a pie and then walk forward to the person who was "it." It was fun because it was almost like imagining that we were eating these pies while playing this game. It made time go by a lot faster. There were other times when all of us would get to play together, and we'd make sort of a train around the room and sing choir songs or pretend that we were a choir ourselves. Then, all together, we would sing a song we heard on the radio. One of our favorites to sing was Kirk Franklin's "Lean on Me." Sometimes we'd make fortresses in our room as best we could with what we had, and we would try to do our homework together or whatever else needed to be done.

Even in bad situations, we would still find ways to play with each other and make each other laugh. We would find ways to eat and find ways to get along, and we'd teach ourselves things that we couldn't learn because we weren't able to go to school that day, or weren't able to go to school that week. We wanted to continue trying to learn something because it gave us something to do—it gave us hope. Catina would often pretend to be our teacher on days that we couldn't go to school. She would have us sit on the floor, and she would read to us and show us other things that she had learned in school. Even though I wasn't good at school (when I was able to go), and I didn't try to be at this point in my life, when I was stuck at home, it seemed like the time to try to learn something and to apply myself, for the sole reason that it gave me something to do.

~

My mom was never disappointed with my grades when they were bad. I guess she just figured I wasn't good at school, and I wasn't smart enough to do anything. Or maybe she felt responsible since I missed so much school, and when I was home, neither she nor Tony would help me with my homework. Mary wasn't a very proactive mom when it came to academia. In fact, I can only remember one time specifically when she came to my school. I remember it because it was for parent-teacher conferences, and I was in front of my friends. My teacher was talking to Mary about how I didn't try, and how I needed to apply myself more, and my mom was talking about how she was going to help me figure out how to behave and do right at school, which I knew meant she was going to beat me. I remember rolling my eyes and pretending that I didn't care what my mom said, pretending that I ran my life, because I was in front of my friends. She saw what I was doing, and she set me straight right in front of everyone by slapping me in the back of the head. My classmates laughed at me, but I straightened up right then and there. I was so scared about going home later that day because I knew she was going to be angry, and I thought that I was going to be in for the beating of a lifetime for disrespecting her like that. But when I got home, she had forgotten all about it, and things were back to normal, or as normal as was possible on a good day in the Bass household.

~

One of the memories that made me feel most loved from my early childhood centers around Parents' Day at my elementary school. This was a day when parents could come and bring their children lunch and eat with them on the school lawn. I remember on this particular day being so overwhelmingly depressed because I knew that I was going to be the only kid that didn't have someone. I figured that with all the beatings I had gotten, Mary couldn't possibly care enough to come to school and bring me lunch. I made my way outside with cafeteria lunch, prepared to sit there alone and trying not to cry in front of everyone. As I looked for a place to sit, I saw my mom and Tony waiting out there with Chinese food for me.

I was so happy at that moment that I completely forgot about all of the starvation, all of the neglect, and all of the beatings that I had received over the years. Then and there, I knew my mom loved me. As they sat there with me eating lunch, I couldn't help but look around, hoping that people were watching me, the proudest kid alive, with my parents. Yes, I was so happy that I even counted Tony as my honorary father. I felt like I had the same kind of family that everyone else had. I felt that our family was normal, and that maybe one day, all of the abuse and neglect would just stop, and maybe we could truly be happy. It is still to this day one of my most cherished memories that I hope never to forget.

What from an adult's perspective looks small and insignificant—one act of having lunch with a child—was huge, and still is huge to me. What an amazing amount of hope that one act of kindness and love created. Their showing up to my school for lunch was enough for me to forget that I was abused on a regular basis, and it gave me a feeling that there was still a chance to come out of the darkness. I can't explain how BIG that little glimpse was, how big all the little bits of fun, kindness, normalcy, were. You cherish them, you hold onto them. You use them as proof that things will improve, that everything will work out, and that it all can change for the better. Those moments are all that you have, and they're so much brighter and bolder because of their scarcity.

SPECIAL

Distinguished or Different from What Is Ordinary or Usual

I remember I used to be very sensitive to teasing and taunting when I was younger, maybe because of all the abuse that I had to endure; maybe it was just my personality. I remember one day at school these kids were making fun of my mom, just randomly, of course. They didn't actually know anything about her, but I started crying. I went home and told my mom about the kind of things they were saying and the jokes they were making, expecting that she would hug me and tell me that it was okay. Instead, she said, "Stop being such a pussy, Jr. Why are you crying about stupid things?"

She then asked me why I would cry instead of fighting back, further insulting my boyhood. Her yelling at me didn't make me feel stronger, though. As one might expect, it did the exact opposite. I felt so weak that I became depressed. I couldn't even do that right. I kept saying to myself, "I guess that's how families are supposed to be. I guess I just need to be tougher. I need to be the man." I figured that was Mary's way of trying to instill some manly qualities in me and make up for the fact that my dad wasn't around. Eventually, those words sunk into my being, and I found myself having difficulty caring about anything with sensitivity. To some extent, I still struggle with allowing myself to feel sadness or sympathy because I can still hear in the farthest recesses of my mind Mary telling me to man up and be tough.

~

There were many times in my childhood when I felt that being the oldest male brought about individualized praise or embarrassment. I found that Mary used to treat me differently than she did the rest of my siblings. I remember Mary telling me when I was younger; that she had a son before she had Catina, but he died as a baby in his bed. I've always wondered if what she said was true or not. I wondered that with a lot of things she said. But she always told me that she wanted to make up for the one that she lost. So, I think that's where I came in for her. I think that I was her chance to make up for losing her first son.

Some days when Mary would make us stay home from school while she worked, she would put me in charge of taking care of everyone else, even Catina, who was older. If we were eating, if there was food in the house, I would be in charge of making breakfast and lunch and sometimes even dinner on the nights when Mary wouldn't come home until really late (if she decided to go out with friends or something). Mary went out a lot. She was gone a lot. And while sometimes we went to daycare or my grandparent's house, we were often home alone. I remember teaching myself how to make scrambled eggs and fried bologna. However, I was still a child and found myself testing the limits of what was acceptable in our family because of the added responsibility.

For example, my mom and Tony used to get specific groceries that only they were allowed to eat, even on occasions when we had our eating privileges. Soda was among the things that we rarely had access to and knew that we were not supposed to touch. On one of the many times my mother left us home for the day, I decided to get into the bottle of Sprite that she had purchased earlier in the week. The bottle was still mostly full, and I knew that she would notice if any was missing, but I couldn't stop myself from sneaking into the kitchen (so that my siblings wouldn't notice) and drinking out of the Sprite bottle. I sneaked into the kitchen several times; each time taking what I believed to be small sips from the forbidden drink. Toward the end of the day, I went back into the kitchen and noticed that the bottle was less than half full, and I began to panic.

There was no way she wouldn't be able to tell that I had gotten into it. And if I was caught, not only would I get a beating, but I also risked losing my place as Mary's go-to child for watching over the house. I had to think quickly. I had to do something, but I wasn't quite sure what that something should be. And then it hit me; water looked the same as Sprite and could probably be used as a substitute, as long as a lot wasn't used. At that moment, I was completely oblivious to the fact that Sprite and water taste completely different and would thus be noticed if substituted. So I filled the bottle back up to where it was in the beginning and prayed that I would get away with my sneakiness since I was clever enough to replace the missing liquid. Later that night, Mary poured herself a glass of the heavily diluted soda and began screaming for us to come downstairs, asking for an explanation as to why her Sprite tasted like water. None of us said anything, mostly because my siblings really had no idea why it tasted like water. After grilling us for a few minutes, Mary gave up and allowed us to go back upstairs to our rooms. I don't know if she just chalked it up to being flat, or if she was trying to show us mercy by not punishing us for a clear violation of her rules, but I was so thankful that we all survived that encounter without harm—especially since I was the only one who was guilty and would truly be deserving of any punishment.

~

Because we were always fearful of harm from my mom if we had disappointed her, we often looked for signs of favor that let us know that she did care about and love us. One of the ways I believed I was seeing favor was through the nickname I was given. Because I was named after my biological father, I was always referred to as Jr. growing up. At this point in my life, I didn't have any real feeling toward my birth father, good or bad, so Jr. was a fine enough name. But eventually, Jr. morphed into June Bug, and that was a name that I loved. I know it sounds weird; after all, who wants to be referred to by the name of an insect, but I loved it. It was something that was just mine. I wasn't as attached to my birth dad, and I believed that nowhere in the world did anyone have a nickname like mine. It was a name that gave me pride and belonging in my family. It helped me believe that I was cared for and special.

~

Even though Larry, Gary, and Jerry were triplets, they all had very different personalities. It was amazing how different they were, and it was so easy to tell them apart all the time. Larry was said to be the oldest, and he was the more sophisticated one. He was always concerned with his looks and liked his hair to be a certain way. He was skinny by nature and had a great personality, and if he were still alive today, he would have had a very bright future. Gary was supposed to be the middle child, and he was the biggest of the three, and I think that he might have had some developmental delays. Still, we all loved being around him because he was always very funny and would make us laugh, no matter what circumstance we found ourselves in. He would just say things that were ridiculous and way out there, but they made sense to him, and he would have us cracking up. He would make up little songs that were so funny because they didn't make any sense. Jerry followed the other two and did what they did, but he was smart enough to know when to be separate from them if they were going to get into trouble. I think maybe his ability to move and mold himself was one of his greatest strengths. He wouldn't openly confront, but he would move or manage himself to survive.

For some reason, my mom didn't see Jerry as being as big a problem as she saw the other two. She went out of her way to make sure that Larry and Gary had miserable lives, even by our family's standards. But Jerry was the exception for some reason, and I really don't know why. But that certainly didn't make his life any easier.

Catina was the only girl, and Mary used to share things with Catina that she wouldn't talk about with the rest of us. When she was upset or needed a confidante, she would share her feelings with Catina. My sister had a special place in my mom's twisted heart that the rest of us could never come close to filling. She was the only girl—the only person who could understand certain aspects of Mary's personality, and that made her very special to Mary.

Catina used to be really into her schoolwork. She wanted to make sure that she got the best grades. I could never understand why she was so invested in school when we spent so much time locked in our bedrooms worrying about when the next meal would come. But every opportunity she had, she tried to use to learn something new: to add another skillset to her being. She held herself to a very high standard and would not tolerate anything less than perfection. I remember her getting a bad grade once that devastated her. As a result, she felt she needed to punish herself, and decided the best way to do that was to cut off her beautiful long hair. But that was Catina. Her emotions were very similar to mine in that they ran pretty high. The difference was that I was easily upset by people hurting my feelings and showed little fear toward actual dangers (with the exception of my mom and Tony).

I remember the babysitter bringing us home from church one time during a pretty bad thunderstorm and Catina freaking out because she hated the sound of thunder and all of the flashes of lightning. Whether it was thunderstorms or doctor's visits, when Catina was scared of something, she made it known and didn't care what kind of scene she made while doing so. I, on the other hand, always tried to hide my emotions and fears, worried that showing such things would disgust my mom.

I think that was one of the biggest differences between Catina and me. As I sat in the car trying to drown out Catina's hysteria, I kept thinking about how utterly fascinated I was by the chaos of the thunderstorm: all of the trees and debris flying around, and rain pouring all around us as if to create the second great flood. Even to this day, with everything that has happened in my life, that kind of chaos still excites me. I am able to find peace in chaotic situations, because that is how my body and mind have adapted. There came a certain ability to ground myself where I stood in order to be able to withstand being swept away with the debris.

Anything that's chaotic gets my blood boiling, gets me energized, and I get a certain hyperactive response to it. It's one of my body's defenses that keeps me from cowering into a corner when things get a little out of hand. Instead, I get excited and motivated to study the problem and see how to solve it. When I look at thunderstorms, I imagine the sky is me and that the sky is normally peaceful. But then disaster comes over it, and instead of letting the disaster take over forever, the sky always overcomes the storm and returns all things in its power to the way they were. I love thunderstorms because I know they have to end. When I look at the sky, I know that it won't always be chaos and that the storm will go away. That's a comforting feeling because, for some people, the storm is the end; there is no coming back from it. There is no sunshine afterwards. It's just storm and then everlasting nothingness.

CREATIVE

Characterized by Sophisticated Bending of the Rules or Conventions, as in Creative Accounting

Although we were a poor family, there were several times in my childhood living with Mary when we were able to afford to have pets. One of those pets was a beautiful white rabbit that I believe came to be a member of our family because the previous owner was tired of it. I remember how its whiskers tickled my hand as it nibbled the food I gave it. But that is about all I can remember of the rabbit's short time as a member of the Bass family, because the day came when we didn't have any food in the house, my mom was out of food stamps, and something had to be done. I vaguely remember watching as my mom took the rabbit out of its cage and left the room. That was to be the last time we would ever see the rabbit. We did get to eat that night, though. After we were done eating, Mary told us she had cooked our rabbit and fed it to us. I don't know if that's true, or if she actually sold it for food money, but I remember thinking at the time that although we had just eaten the rabbit, it wasn't all that gross. I was that hungry. I remember thinking, "This is the best thing I've ever eaten," and, "Maybe we should buy more rabbits if that means we get to eat." But Mary would often tell us stories like that—stories that were meant to break our spirits. I don't know if she thought it would hurt us and told us about killing and cooking the rabbit just to get a response, or if she just didn't care. Maybe she thought it would toughen us up, knowing how far people have to go in order to take care of family. I guess she figured being honest with us couldn't possibly do any more damage than what she was already doing. And if it did, she didn't seem concerned.

~

During the times when we were starved, we used to try to bring food home from school. We used to have rations, and if we ate lunch, and it was something that we could wrap up, such as an apple or something that we could put in our pockets, we would try to because we didn't know if we were going to eat when we got home. I remember having this Chicago Bulls coat that was so old and worn out that it had several holes in the lining. I would stuff food into the ripped parts of the inside of my coat so that I would have a snack to eat when I got home. I stole lots of food from the cafeteria and put it in my coat for safekeeping as I finished out the school day. Once I got home, I would hide it in my closet underneath my dirty clothes. Because we did laundry infrequently, it was a pretty safe bet that we would be able to hide food for long periods of time under unwashed clothing. And without toys or dressers, it was really the only option we had available to us. Then, if we wouldn't eat that night, I would wait until Mom and Tony went to sleep, and I'd have Larry, Gary, Jerry, and Catina come into my room and split up the food that I'd gotten. We would have what we liked to call our "feasts."

There were times when Larry, Gary, and Jerry also did the same thing. They stole loaves of hamburger and hot dog buns, and loaves of other bread, because the bread truck would come to their school while they were there. I don't know how they managed to steal stuff from the truck, but they did. So, they stole all these loaves of bread, and I mean we had lots of bread. We stuck it in Catina's closet because it was the biggest, and she also had the most clothing in her room and on her closet floor. We would hide food in there and would make trips to our self-made food bank periodically to cover missed meals. We tried to conserve our stash, save it for as long as possible, because we didn't know when we'd be able to eat. Unfortunately, the bread wouldn't stay edible forever, and after we tried to eat around the mold, and sometimes through the mold, we would have to find ways to discard what remained. That was probably one of the hardest things to do—throw out food. In a way, it was as if we were helping Mary and Tony seal our fate of starving to death.

~

Mary was very good at giving us hope that we could be happy before taking it away. When she got bored with dangling food in front of us, or thought that her threats of beating weren't doing the trick, she would try to come up with other ways to make us miserable. One time, she got mad at us for something she thought we did wrong, and she told us that we were grounded for the whole year. In order to properly implement the grounding, she told us that all of our toys were going to be thrown into the trash. She had us take all of the toys we had, which weren't very many, to begin with, put them in trash bags, and throw them in the dumpster in front of our house. So, for a year, we had no toys, we couldn't watch TV, and we had to stay upstairs in our rooms. There were times where she slipped and let us watch TV or come out of our rooms to go outside. This was especially the case if she had to go to work and didn't want us to go to school. On those days, Mary would let us sit downstairs all day and watch TV and even allowed us to decide what to eat while she was gone. For the most part, however, we were grounded for an entire year: doing absolutely nothing and left to play whatever imaginary games we could think of with each other. But at this point, I figured there wasn't a whole lot more she could do to surprise or torment us. I would soon find out that I was very wrong in that assumption.

~

Occasionally, my mom would use her creative powers for good and would do everything in her power to help us fit in with peers our age, as seen in a specific school Halloween party that my class was having. Kids were supposed to bring costumes, so they could dress up at the end of the day when we would go to different classrooms for trick-or-treating. This was to be followed by a costume party, where kids and their parents would enjoy snacks that each classmate had brought. Well, money was tight in our family (as usual), and my mom didn't want to buy a Halloween costume for me just so I could walk around school and wear it once. So, instead of buying me a costume, she decided to make me one out of her hair weave that she hadn't been using. She took the weave and hair glue and attached all of the fake hair to my arms, ankles, and parts of my face, making me a "scary werewolf." So, all day I had to walk around my school, itchy and embarrassed with fake hair attached to my body. People laughed at me because I had this ghetto weave costume on that I was forced to wear all day, drawing the attention of everyone who had brought costumes that could be changed into when the time came. And there I was, stuck as a werewolf, thanks to my cheap, ghetto mom. I hated her for making me go to school like that, and everyone knew what a weave looked like, so they could all tell that I was covered in it. It wasn't a fun experience then, but now that I'm older, it's kind of a funny story, and I see the creativity in it.

Birthdays and Christmases were always mysteries living with Mary because we never knew what we were going to get, if anything. We never knew if you were going to have an actual birthday, or if it was going to be her simply saying "Happy Birthday!" and that's it. For my tenth birthday, I remember Tony, along with his kids from his previous marriage, and Mary, and all of my siblings going to a park to have a picnic. Then we went home and had root beer floats with Cheetos to dip into them. Mary told me that she had planned to get me a TV for my birthday present, but she couldn't afford it, so instead, she told me that my birthday present for that year was that she was going to allow me to curse in the house and not get in trouble for it. I was so happy. I went around the rest of the day saying "Shit" whenever I did something like stub my toe, or I'd purposely get mad and say "Damn." I made the most of it. But there were still limits. Mom told me that her only rule was that "I couldn't cuss at her," that if I cussed at her, she would "kill me." I would have never pushed it that far. Not in a million years. I didn't need her to tell me that; I knew she would. She meant it.

My mom used to make threats like that all the time, though. She used to say things like, "I brought you into this world, I can take you out." And for us boys, she especially wanted us to be scared; she didn't want us to think that we were ever going to get too big for her. She used to say, "You have one hit, and if it doesn't kill me, I'll kill you." Because sometimes we'd get so mad, we wouldn't care that we were going to get beaten. We'd just get mad and would give her the same death glare that she would give us. When she would see us give her that look, it would almost be like she was taunting us with her own glare, saying, "Hit me if you want, but I guarantee you it will be the last thing that you ever do." And of course, none of us were ever stupid enough to try it. We weren't big enough yet, and honestly, even if we were big enough, we still would have had enough respect and fear of her to ever try acting on our anger. There were times when I just wanted to knock her across the head, but then, I flashed forward to how my life would end, and I figured it wasn't worth it. I wonder now, how many 6-, 8-, or 10-year-olds actually consider their own death at the hands of their parents. Whatever the number, I know from my experience in social services that it is far too large.

My mom could be really caring one day, and then switch characters the next. Sometimes she switched in the middle of a day. She would go from being happy to being angry. The times when she seemed sanest occurred when she was single and on her own, and could actually be a mother. When she got a boyfriend, then it became stressful and too much for her. At least, that is how I interpreted events. When we were little and living with Mary, it didn't seem that she was crazy. I mean, we just thought that we were either really bad or that's just how families worked. We couldn't really see that there was something wrong with her.

I do know that Mary always fully understood what she was doing. If she was ever "not crazy," I didn't notice since her personality was always so sporadic. I think we always had to deal with her being not right in the head: her rage, anger, and changing moods. The degree of the behavior changed, and the severity seemed more intense when she was involved with someone. But maybe it was just that there was less of the positive. That energy went to whomever she was dating. The only thing that really noticeably changed was the starvation. Food and money were always scarce before. Food was used as a reward or a punishment. But her consciously, intentionally starving us really was more of a thing that came toward the end of our time with her. In the beginning when we didn't eat, it was because she couldn't afford to give us food. I think after she saw how that affected us, she began to use it as a method of control.

EDUCATE

To Develop or Train

Two of Three Triplets Died from Abuse
Posted: Saturday, October 23, 1999
By CRAIG HORST
The Associated Press

KANSAS CITY, Mo. — People just knew something was wrong in the two-story house on the corner at the top of a small rise in the quiet neighborhood.

But no one suspected the horror of two 8-year-old boys—two-thirds of a set of triplets—being starved and burned with scalding water until they finally died.

The thought of one of the boys weighing less than 30 pounds when he was found unconscious by his mother Wednesday night has led to sleepless nights among the neighbors and shocked even a veteran homicide investigator.

The mother of the boys, Mary Bass, was in court Friday to hear the 10 charges of assault, abuse and neglect just hours after the second boy died.

An innocent plea was entered for her as she trembled and mumbled to herself. Other charges could be filed when a coroner's report is received, Jackson County Prosecutor Robert Beaird said.

"I haven't slept for two nights," said Maxine Thomas, who has lived two houses down from the corner house for 22 years. "The little girl across the street from them hasn't slept for two nights. She looks terrible. The whole neighborhood is devastated."

Bass, her boyfriend, and their five children had moved in about a year ago. But people hardly saw them.

"I never laid eyes on her," Thomas said. "The man, he was introduced to me when they first moved in. He looked like a real nice man. But I never saw him again."

Bass called 911 Wednesday night after finding one of the boys, Larry, unconscious in the living room. He died in the house.

Gary was taken to the hospital in critical condition and died early Friday.

"It was just a skeletal structure. There was no muscle mass," Capt. Darryl Forte, commander of the homicide unit, said of Larry. "It was like something in a Third World country. It's just not something you want to see in this country."

Bass, who told police the boys were discipline problems, apparently locked them in an upstairs bedroom for days at a time, feeding them bread and water and letting them out only to use the bathroom.

Bass told police it was difficult to work full time and go back to school while trying to raise the five children. When she had trouble controlling two of the triplets, she apparently began withholding food this past summer.

Teachers began seeing signs of neglect as long as two years ago, and they alerted state social workers.

The Missouri Division of Family Services declined to discuss the family's case or say if it had investigated.

"I thought something was strange," Thomas said. "But I couldn't put my finger on it. I'm not a nosy person. When you live alone, you try to keep to yourself."

The children were rarely seen outside playing, and when they were, they weren't allowed to go outside the fence around the front yard. Apparently, only one of the triplets attended school regularly.

"I never have seen a couple of the boys," said A.J. Madden, Thomas' ex-husband who was helping her bring her flower pots in for the winter. "I saw the girl a few times. They just kept to themselves."

The three surviving children—a 12-year-girl, a 10-year-old boy and the surviving triplet, Jerry—were found to be in good shape when they were taken to the hospital. They were immediately placed in foster care, Forte said.

"They were OK," Forte said. "They weren't shocked. They weren't screaming or anything when we told them we were going to take them. In the girl's room, she had some books spread out with a notebook and a pencil like she had been studying."

The living room of the house was furnished, but three bedrooms had little furniture, Forte said. Three mattresses were found -- one downstairs and two in upstairs bedrooms, he said.

The street of bungalows and two-story houses had well-kept lawns, although several were in need of a raking of fall leaves on a sunny fall day. Only the yard at the corner house seemed neglected.

It was quiet, although it is only about three blocks from the traffic of one of the city's major streets, Independence Boulevard, a street lined with fast-food restaurants, discount furniture stores and pawn shops northeast of downtown.

Thomas said she was thinking about moving from her tidy, little home.

"I'm going to have to go down to my farm for a little while," she said. "I can't take this. This is terrible. This is a tragedy. If we would have known they needed help, we would have helped them. I know everyone would have helped the children."[v]

What I liked best about being at Faxon Montessori was that I was treated the same as everyone else, even though I had troubles with learning. The teachers didn't make me feel like an outcast, even though I had to have extra help in certain subjects, like reading. As an adult, I'm not sure that is such a good thing, but back then, normal was all I wanted.

There was this teacher, Ms. Washington, who used to come in a couple of times a week and individually take students into the hall to have us practice reading to her. I remember that most of the times I went out there to read to her, I'd be trying to figure out how to read a certain page, and she would be sleeping through it. She was out like a light. I'd have to try to wake her up if there was a word I didn't know or couldn't figure out. After a while, I just gave up on it and just started skipping over words, and skipping over the book, and getting done much quicker than I would have if I was really reading. She would pretend that she was awake for the whole thing and let me go back into the classroom.

My leadership skills that developed as a result of being charged with watching over my siblings at home led me to believe that I was the ideal leader for my group of friends at school. The group of friends that I "led" used to go around and pretend that we were part of this karate gang, serving justice to the rest of the playground. One time, this kid Christian was messing with my best friend, Aniseto, and he came up to me asking for help. So, as leader, I went to fight this bully, securing my place as group leader. What started as yelling and name-calling turned into an actual fistfight as we were going back up the stairs to the classroom. It didn't take long for the teachers to intervene and separate us, sending as to the principal's office to have our punishment decided. As we walked to the office together, not even halfway there, we were already back to being friends. When we got to the principal's office, nothing really serious happened to us since we were already cool with each other and we had calmed down. Peace was restored to the group and the playground, and I was able to show my friends that I had their backs, which was not something I felt I was always able to show my siblings.

School was just about the only place where my siblings and I had different experiences. Because we all went to different schools, there were times when we would try and impress each other with tales of what happened in our day. We used to tell stories about how certain teachers at school would take us, by ourselves, to get food from certain restaurants. While we all knew it wasn't really true, there were times when I would tell them that one of my teachers took me to McDonald's and fed me all the food that I wanted, and that she didn't care what I ordered. Or I would brag about how I got to eat that day because my teacher took me to "this place." Catina, along with the rest of them, would tell the same type of stories. We would make up those stories to make ourselves feel better and to make it seem as though we got special treatment outside of the house. It was a way for us to live out fantasies that there were adults in the world who wanted to take care of us. We'd feel that at least somebody in this world cared about us, if only for a few minutes. I think we all knew in the back of our heads that each of us was lying, but when we told those stories, it gave us hope and made us feel happy.

~

Although I lived to make Mary proud of me and relished the opportunity to show how mature I was when she asked me to look after my siblings, I was still a child, and I struggled with always following my mom's directions exactly how she wanted. I remember one such time when Catina and I were charged with making sure my brother, Jerry, got off the bus safely since Mary had to work late. Well, it was a particularly hot day, so Catina and I figured we would go to a nearby Sonic to grab slushies with some change we had because we still had time before Jerry's bus was supposed to arrive at his stop. As we were walking back, I remember seeing our mom walking toward us, and I began freaking out. She was extremely angry with us because apparently, Jerry had gotten off the bus already and had no one there to walk him the block or so from the stop to our house. Luckily, my grandpa had been able to pick my mom up from work and drop her off in time to meet Jerry along his trek home.

I remember her walking us back home, and screaming at us the entire way for everyone in the neighborhood to hear. There were a couple of kids playing outside of their house, and I remember them watching with eyes wide open as Mary laid into us. Because I was so embarrassed that everyone was watching me get in trouble, I tried to make it look like it was only Catina being reprimanded by shaking my head as if I were disappointed in the bad choice she made. Of course, my mom saw it, and she popped me in the back of the head, causing the neighbor kids to burst into laughter. There were lots of times where I tried to make it look like I could get away with things that I knew I couldn't, but it was worth it at the time, because I didn't want to be embarrassed in front of kids that I had to see. Mary threatened to beat us when we got to the house, but that time, she didn't go through with it. We thought that for the first time, we had escaped a fated punishment.

Then it must have been a month later, as we were just sitting upstairs, minding our own business and trying not to make much noise, when Mary called all five of us down to the living room. We thought that maybe we were getting some food or some sort of treat since we were being good. She proceeded to tell us that she had been storing up the things we had done, so that in one day she could beat all of us for it. She then told us that the reason she called us downstairs was because it was now time to receive that beating. She had us line up in the kitchen from youngest to oldest, and told us that we would be called into the living room one at a time to get our beatings with the extension cord.

While waiting for my turn, I kept telling Catina that maybe we should run away in order to avoid being beaten. It was one of the only times that I remember actually thinking about escaping my mom permanently. As our turn got closer and closer, we became more convinced that making a run for it was the best option. Unfortunately, we never mustered up the courage because we knew that ultimately, whoever found us would bring us back to Mary, and the beating would be even worse. So we waited for our turn, growing increasingly more anxious with every sound of the extension cord hitting the skin of my brother who had gone before me. Hearing the sounds of my siblings screaming and begging for Mary to stop hitting them was almost worse than getting the actual beating. Those screams are what remain in my memories all these years later. It hurts my soul, every fiber of my being, to think about the people I loved begging for relief from torment.

Finally, my turn came, and my heart began to race. I remember walking into the living room and seeing what looked like water on the ground. Mary saw me looking at the spot and told me that one of my brothers had peed all over himself due to the fear and pain of being beaten. After getting my beating, I went upstairs, and I started cursing at Mary and saying how much I hated her, and how I wanted her to get hit by a bus. Then Catina came up, and she was crying as hard as I was, and we talked about how much we hated Mary. We started plotting ways to kill her. Soon, the crying turned to laughing, because the ways we thought up were so funny. We had snot running from our noses; when we laughed suddenly, we made snot bubbles that would make us laugh even harder. Even though we'd just gotten beaten, beaten so hard that we couldn't sit down, we still found something that was funny and something that we could laugh at and share with each other.

Our beatings were so regular by this time that if we didn't find some way to laugh, we would have surely given up on trying to live. I strongly believe that we wouldn't have lasted much longer if we couldn't find something to hold onto in our lives. And thinking of ways we could kill my mom was one of the funniest and most distracting things we could do.

~

Catina once ran away from school. I remember all of us being freaked out because we didn't know where she was. We went up to Northeast, where she went to school, and the police were there, and we were looking for her, and no one could find her anywhere. We were all worried. After a while, we couldn't do any more at the school, and so we came home, and she was sitting on the back porch. Just sitting there. I thought our mom was going to beat her to death, but she didn't. She ran and hugged her and then yelled at her about how she couldn't just run away if she was having problems at school, and then they cried together. It was one of the rare non-beating parenting moments that I saw from Mary. She didn't try to kill Catina or anything like that. She was scared that she'd lost her child and wouldn't see her again, and she was relieved when Catina was waiting for us.

It was one of those types of moments that would give us hope— one of those "see, we're just a normal family" moments. It was so comforting. These moments made us feel whatever love she had for us, and made us feel we were connected.

~

We used to have to write a journal entry every week or every day at Faxon, and I remember towards the end, when it got really bad at home, I told a girl named Brittany what was happening to me. I told her that we were getting beaten and starved and things like that, but I made her promise not to tell anyone. And she didn't tell; she kept my secret. After my brothers died, I came back to school, and my teacher was telling me how Brittany felt so guilty because she had kept that from everyone, and that she kept thinking that maybe if she had told someone, it would have helped me and maybe things would have turned out differently. It actually kind of hurt our friendship, because she was always so sad that she really couldn't be around me very much or look at me without feeling guilty.

EVIL

Morally Wrong or Bad; Immoral; Wicked: An Evil Life

BC-TRIPLET DEATH-KAN
Starve-Abuses Second Triplet in Abuse Case Dies
(For use by New York Times News Service clients)
By CHRISTINE VENDEL

KANSAS CITY, Mo. — Eight-year-old Gary Bass died at a hospital early Friday, two days after police found him and his brother, both emaciated and burned, inside their northeast Kansas City home.

His brother, Larry Bass, was pronounced dead Wednesday night at the house. Gary was rushed to a hospital, but died about 2:15 a.m. Friday.

The boys were triplets. The other triplet and two other siblings who lived at the house were not abused, police said. The three surviving children have been placed in protective custody.

The boys' mother, Mary L. Bass, 31, was charged Thursday with 10 felonies for allegedly abusing Larry and Gary. The charges didn't include murder and were not upgraded after Gary's death because prosecutors were waiting for the medical examiner's report on Larry and Gary.

"At that time, we will see if the charges need to be modified," said Jackson County Prosecutor Bob Beaird. "In any case, you need to have a cause of death established scientifically." Beaird said he expected the medical examiner's reports early next week.

Because the boys' bodies will not be released by the medical examiner until the reports are finished, funeral arrangements have not been made. Alvin Brooks, president of the Ad Hoc Group Against Crime, said Friday that he had called Mary Bass to ask whether any family members could arrange the funeral.

Bass told him that her father, who lives in Kansas City, could help, but she did not know that Gary had died. Brooks said he had to tell her. She then asked him if he would visit her in jail.

Brooks and others met with her for about 40 minutes late Friday afternoon. She asked Brooks to call her supervisor at the Federal Aviation Administration to tie up some loose ends.

And she asked him to get apple cider and soda pop to her older children for their school Halloween parties next week, Brooks said.

The alleged abuse at the Bass home was brought to the attention of police about 7:25 p.m. Wednesday, when Mary Bass found Larry unresponsive and called the police. When officers arrived, they saw Gary was sick, too.

Court records say Mary Bass told police that, to discipline the boys, she had locked them in a bedroom for up to two weeks at a time, feeding them only bread and water and allowing them out for restroom breaks. Last Friday, the boys' feet were dunked in scalding water, court records said. The wounds went untreated except for some ointment and gauze pads, police said.

All five of Mary Bass' children shared the name Bass, but the siblings had different fathers. Relatives said Mary Thomas, her maiden name, met Ronald Bass in high school and later became pregnant, giving birth to a daughter in early 1987. She and Bass married in May 1987 and had a son two years later. She then dated another man and became pregnant with the triplets. Ronald stayed with Mary and treated the triplets as his own, said his mother, Gloria Bass of Kansas City.

Ronald and Mary divorced when the triplets were about 2. Ronald moved to Fort Wayne, Ind., Gloria Bass said.

A judge ordered Ronald to pay $365 in child support each month, but it was not clear Friday whether he complied. Gloria Bass said her son last saw his children and the triplets when he was in town last year.

"They stayed here with me for a week," she said. "All of them."

Mary Bass earned a certificate in accounting from Penn Valley Community College, police said. In 1997, she got a job with the FAA. An agency spokesman, Tony Molinaro, said she had started as a secretary in the civil-rights office, but transferred to the Flight Standards Division last year.

In December 1998, Mary Bass bought a four-bedroom, 2-story house for $58,000. The house was kept clean and neat, but sparse: Police said all the furnishings could fit into one room.

Brooks said Mary Bass' career prospects were looking up, but her home life was troubled. Mary Bass also told police she had trouble juggling the demands of a full-time job, going to school and raising five children.

Homicide Capt. Darryl Forte said Mary Bass told them she had talked with Division of Family Services workers several times. It was not clear what action, if any, was taken after the meetings.

Deb Hendricks, a spokeswoman for the division, said the court has ordered Bass' three remaining children put into foster care. But she said state law prohibits her from saying whether the division ever had contact with the Bass family.

The triplets were enrolled at Swinney Elementary School this year, but officials said only Jerry Bass attended regularly. The school principal referred questions to the central district office. No one was available there to say whether the school reported Larry's and Gary's absences or whether any of the siblings showed signs of abuse. But the mother of one student said classmates commented on how skinny one Bass child was.

Teachers and other school officials are required to report suspected child abuse to the state Division of Family Services.

Jeanne Jones, Jackson County children services director, said her agency is evaluating whether her staff acted appropriately.

"If for any reason our staff didn't do what it should have, we'll take appropriate action," Jones said. "That could involve more staff training all the way up to termination."

Both boys' deaths also will be the subject of a Child Fatality Review Panel, Jones said. The panel, which includes social workers, prosecutors and advocacy groups, looks for ways to prevent similar incidents.

Because nothing else seemed to work, police said, she resorted to withholding food as discipline. Police said severe food restrictions began this summer.

According to police and court records, the boys would be fed only bread and water for up to two weeks at a time. Once, when one of the boys was caught stealing food, they were locked in a room, where the starvation continued, records said. They would be let out only to use the bathroom, the records said, and would stay locked up all day while Bass was at work.

Last week, court records allege, Bass became enraged at Larry and Gary and dipped their feet in a tub of scalding water. Their skin was burned off in places. Police said the boys' feet looked as though they had on blood-red socks.

Bass and her 36-year-old live-in boyfriend said they had not sought medical attention for the boys because they were afraid they would be arrested, according to a detective's affidavit. The boyfriend has not been charged.

Towards the end, another thing changed. My mom had always put me in charge of things; I think because I was the oldest male in our family. She would sometimes talk to me and interact with me and not the rest of my siblings. She would have me cook dinner, or have me get things for her. When I was eight or nine years old, I started to notice that my mom treated me differently, because I realized that I wasn't getting punished as severely. I wasn't starving as much as everyone else was, and things weren't as bad for me.

But the shift now was that she would make me decide how the others should be punished, and what should happen to them, and if she didn't like my idea, she would tell me to think about it more. I think now that this was a unique form of torture.

She would still get mad at me and would beat me too, but my punishments weren't always as severe as the triplets' were. But if she was going to beat everyone, I was right along with them. I don't think I got beat as often, and toward the end, it seemed like hardly ever at all. It was the same for Catina. She had a special bond with Catina as well, since Catina was her only girl. But, for some reason, it just didn't seem as strong as the bond I had with my mom.

Then toward the very end, being her "favorite" also meant that I was the one who had to carry out a punishment if she didn't want to do it. Towards the very end, right before my two brothers died, I remember my mom used to have me beat Larry and Gary for her.

That's the one thing that I still feel horribly guilty about today. But, at the time, it was either beat them, or get beaten myself, and when it came to survival, I just did what I had to do. There was no other option for me. There was no way I could say to Mary, "Well, this makes me uncomfortable, so I'm not going to do it." That would not have flown with her and would have just resulted in me getting beaten right along with them and probably harder because it meant that I had disobeyed a direct order from her. It wasn't like she was giving me a suggestion; it was a demand, and a demand I had to follow. I didn't see any way that the situation would possibly end well or how I could possibly get out of doing what she demanded— even if what she demanded was for me to beat two people I loved— two people who played a major role in my staying alive. Two people, who along with Jerry and Catina, were my whole world. My little brothers, whom I knew I should protect—I was now the one causing them pain.

As I looked at these two helpless starving boys, their eyes full of sadness from the kind of life they had to live, I kept wanting to have the strength to take their place. I wanted to be able to turn to Mary and say, "That's enough! Stop picking on my brothers." I wanted to turn to this woman, this cruel woman with the look of pure amusement in her eyes and on her face as she thought about how she was making me do her dirty work, and I wanted to start beating her. I wanted to get the triplets and Catina to join me in beating that satisfied look off of her face. But I realized that I was still small, still just as powerless as I was on the day I had to watch Roosevelt hurt her without being able to do anything. "Why do I have to be such a coward?" was a question that I often asked myself. "Why can't I tap into that same crazy that is in Mom to give her a taste of her own medicine?" I wanted to be strong, I wanted to stand up for what was right, but I couldn't.

I don't know how this sounds, but I truly believed with every fiber of my being that death was close by, and any wrong turn could be my last. A wrong turn could turn out to be all of our last. Walking on eggshells doesn't describe it.

So, I did as she commanded. I beat them for her.

I tried not to hit them as hard as Mary would have. I tried to go as easy on them as I could, but she would stay in the room and watch me, and if I wasn't doing it brutally enough, she would yell at me, "Hit them harder. Or do you want me to do it?" She knew what she was having me do. She knew that I was breaking into pieces over this horrifying position she was forcing me into. She was thrilled by the thought of turning me against them; thrilled with her new form of torture. What better way to make someone suffer than at the hands of one of the people trying to protect them? It was the hardest thing I've ever had to do, the hardest thing I've forced myself to do. And the worst mistake of my life, though I'm not sure there was a choice to make.

I think it makes it even harder now, but they never hated me afterwards. It was just the way the house was run. We didn't fight with each other because of it. No one glared at me, or tormented me, or asked me, "How could you?" They understood, even if I didn't, even if no one else on the planet could. We lived in the same world. They understood.

The only thing we fought over at that point was food. Wanting food, wanting to have each other's food, that would make us fight. There were times when we would threaten to tell on each other if we didn't get what we wanted—if we thought someone owed us a portion of food. We threatened to tell, even though we knew that if we had gone downstairs to tell Tony or Mary, we would just get beaten and then none of us would have gotten to eat. For food, we'd do almost anything. Negotiate, trade, threaten. Food was all that mattered at that point. Even the beatings didn't really matter.

POINT OF NO RETURN

The Critical Point in an Undertaking, Decision-Making Process, etc., Where One Has Committed Oneself Irrevocably to a Course of Action or Policy

... As a result of the prosecutions, authorities learned Bass and Dixon had deceived Johnson about Larry's and Gary's whereabouts. On August 17, 1999, Larry and Gary were not living with their natural father, nor were they visiting their grandparents. Instead, sometime before Johnson arrived, Bass and Dixon locked Larry and Gary in the basement, bound their hands and feet together with rope, and gagged their mouths with socks. Bass and Dixon threatened the other three children with starvation and beatings if they told Johnson the truth about their brothers' treatment or their whereabouts. [vi]

The next social worker that came out, as I remember, was toward the end of everything—just before my two brothers died. I remember that at this point in time, my mom had started locking Larry and Gary in the basement where she would tie them up like dogs. When the social worker arrived, one of the first things that she asked was where Larry and Gary were. My mom told her they were with their biological father, and the social worker believed her and didn't press the issue any further. Little did she know that the two boys she was asking about were in the basement right below her, tied and gagged so that they could not scream for help. The social worker never left the front room.

I remember, right before the social worker came, my mom was making some kind of stew, and she had told us that if we lied and cooperated and did what we were supposed to do, then we would get to eat what she was making. How I hated her at that moment, hate her now when I remember it. I was torn between getting fed and saving my brothers. And almost as if my mom knew that one of us might try to be a hero, she said with such a calm tone of voice that it scared me more than the fear of being beaten, "Even if one of you does say something to make her take you from me, she will have to leave to go get the police first, and in that time, who knows what might happen to you." As she said this, she continued cooking with a look on her face that showed how clever she thought she was. She saw that we were very hungry, so she fed us a little snack beforehand so that we could make it through the questioning from the social worker.

So we said whatever lie came to our heads about how everything was great, and we'd make up stories about places we would go with our mom, all of which were completely untrue. We talked about the different foods we got to eat, and how we always had groceries, and made up other lies. Yet if the social worker had taken the time and actually did a thorough investigation, she would have been able to see right through it all.

Once again, this social worker also questioned us in front of my mom. Even at my age, I knew that was weird. How crazy were they to expect us to be able to feel free to open up when the person against whom these allegations had been made was right in the room with us? Even if they did decide to do something, we weren't sure when they would do it. We were terrified that the social worker would have to leave and get some additional help before she could come back, and we didn't want to think about all of the things that Mary could have done to us before the social worker got back. Also, we had heard horrible things about what happened to kids who were taken away. We knew that the safest thing was to not cross

Mary, particularly when it was so important, and she was acting as if this was important. So, we just said and did whatever we could to stay alive and to get fed for the day.

SNAP

To Break Suddenly, Especially with a Sharp, Cracking Sound, as Something Slender and Brittle: The Branch Snapped

Two months after DFS closed the Bass file, Bass forced Larry and Gary to submerge their feet and lower legs into scalding bath water, causing severe burns. On October 20, 1999, Kansas City police, fire, and emergency medical technicians responded to a 911 call made from the Bass home. State v. Bass, 81 S.W.3d 595, 599 (Mo.Ct.App.2002). Upon arrival, emergency personnel observed Bass kneeling on the living room floor near Larry, who was lifeless, emaciated, and naked except for a pair of socks. After paramedics declared Larry dead, they proceeded upstairs, where they discovered Gary, emaciated and lying on a vomit-stained mattress. En route to the emergency room, the paramedics removed Gary's socks and discovered third-degree burns on his feet and lower legs, several gangrene toes, and multiple abrasions on his back. Despite intensive medical treatment, Gary died two days later.

To ascertain their causes of death, autopsies were performed on the boys. At death, Larry measured 45 inches and weighed 31 pounds; Gary measured 47 inches and weighed 32 pounds. Id. The autopsies revealed the boys died from starvation and bacteria-infected thermal burns to their legs and feet. The autopsy reports classified both deaths as homicides. [vii]

Toward the end of my two brothers' lives, my mom decided she didn't want to put them in the basement anymore. We had this very small broom cupboard that would barely hold a broom, a mop, and a bucket. My mom kept that stuff in there, and put Larry and Gary in there as well. And that was where they would stay all day. And that was where they slept at night, standing up. They weren't able to lie down. And they weren't able to sit down at the same time. They had to sit on each other and try to find ways to be comfortable. We could hear them crawling and climbing around trying to find a way to rest. Near the end, they got so skinny that they were actually able to maneuver it, so they could sit in that cramped space. There was extra room in the closet because they were so small.

I remember coming home from school one day, and mom told me that she was so angry at them because they had gotten out the night before. The broom closet was right in the kitchen, so they got out and were climbing on the counters to get food and take it back into the closet with them. Of course, they were caught. Mary decided to feed them dog food that day for their punishment. She said, "Oh they wanna' act like dogs, huh? Well, I'll treat them like dogs." She then proceeded to tell us about how they had vomited when she first made them eat dog food and how she then made them eat their vomit too.

She then began to laugh. She started giving me a look that suggested she wanted me to laugh with her and approve of what she did to them. I mustered a smile on the outside, but on the inside, I wanted to hit her with a frying pan. I wanted to be sick.

How could I love someone that was so evil? How could I have wanted to protect someone who had such little regard for other peoples' lives? I hated myself, wishing that I could go back in time and help Roosevelt beat her, or that I would have encouraged Tony to strangle every bit of life out of her. At that moment, I told myself she no longer deserved to live.

Later that night, Mary made us a meal with mashed potatoes. I remember her grinding up more dog food and sticking it on their plates and then made Larry and Gary eat it, telling them that "If they want to act like animals, they would be fed like them." It was just really hard to watch.

But at that moment, something started to snap in me. At the same time that I hated her, I was starting to become so brainwashed that I began to think that maybe they deserved what was happening to them. I began thinking that maybe they were really bad because the rest of us weren't getting in that much trouble. Even Jerry, who was their triplet, wasn't getting in that much trouble.

I didn't want to believe that she was just being abusive to them for no reason. I don't know why, but that would be even more terrifying. Even after I had just felt so much hatred for her, it subsided, and I went back to behaving like a loyal soldier following every order that was given to me, even what I was supposed to think.

~

A few days later, literally starving to death, they got out of the closet and got food, and they got caught in the act. My mom caught them and beat them and locked them back in the cupboard. A couple of days later, my mom told me to go run hot bath water in the tub upstairs and to make sure that I didn't use any cold water. I just thought she was going to take a bath at first. I was thinking about how strange it was that she was just going to have a hot water bath because I knew that would hurt, but I did as I was told. I remember the steam rising from the bathtub, and I stuck a finger in it to test the temperature, quickly pulling it back out due to the pain. As I turned to the bathroom door, ready to tell my mom that she might want to put cold water in her bath after all, I saw that she had Larry and Gary with her. Before I even knew what was happening, she had them strip off their clothes, and she pushed them into the scalding hot bathtub. The screams from them being burned still resound in my head today if I allow myself to think about it. They were screaming and falling because it was wet and slippery. No matter how they tried to jump, they kept getting burned and falling full body into the water. Anytime they would try to jump out, Mary would push them back in. After a couple of minutes, she had me leave. She told me to get out, and she closed the door.

As I sat with Catina and Jerry outside the bathroom, I could hear them screaming. They were begging for help and promising to be good. Mary was screaming, too. She was angry that they were being loud and ruining her moment. She kept telling them how bad they were, and how they deserved the hot water since they wanted to keep stealing her food.

But their screams of pain and agony were much louder, and Catina, Jerry and I were just standing right outside the door, not knowing what was going on. Not knowing what to do. This had never happened before.

All of a sudden, Mary stopped screaming, and all I could hear were the sobs of Larry and Gary. After a few more minutes, my mom came out, and she had this look on her face like something really, really bad had just happened.

She said that she had really messed up. She kept saying it over and over again. She said, "I really messed up this time." "I really messed up." She then proceeded to walk down the stairs. Shortly after she left, my two brothers came out. An immense feeling of horror took over my body as I watched Larry and Gary walk out of that bathroom with blisters all over their legs, from their toes to the mid-thigh. They were just covered in blisters, and we didn't know what to do, not even what to think. It was bad.

We were really freaked out about what was going to happen next. It never had been this serious before. Was my mom going to call someone? Was she going to take them to the hospital? Were we going to get taken away from her?

Even though we'd been through all of this traumatic stuff, the thought of getting taken away from my mom was just about the scariest thing that I could imagine. We didn't want to go to some people we didn't know. We didn't want to be taken away. Of course, we wanted the abuse to stop, but I had always figured that one day my mom would change, and things would get better. That's what I dreamt of, hoped for, planned for. It wasn't possible, in my mind, that things could possibly get better if we were taken away from her. We knew that would make it all worse. At least together we were a family.

I remember going downstairs and talking to my mom, trying to get a sense of what was going on. She was contemplating whether she should take Larry and Gary to the hospital or not. She almost had herself convinced, and then she realized that they would most likely take her to jail for abuse. She decided not to take them to the doctor, to just leave things as they were. After a while, I went back upstairs, and as I got to the top of the stairs, I saw Larry and Gary sitting in the hallway, in what looked like a pool of water. It looked like the tub had overflowed into the hall, but it hadn't. One look at Catina and Jerry's faces told me that something was horribly, horribly wrong.

Because the pain in their legs was so great, Larry and Gary had peeled the skin off their blistered legs, and all the puss and fluids that had been in the blisters were all over the floor. I had walked up the stairs right after they peeled the last of it off. It was the most horrifying thing I'd ever seen. As I looked on in horror, I couldn't help but feel kind of fascinated at the same time. I was amazed that fluids like that were in a human body. I wanted to know how those fluids came about. It makes me wonder, now, if I was that much like my mom that I could see the "coolness" in something that was so awful. It just seemed so unreal. I didn't know that that's how a body worked, and it looked like they had just shed their skin. It was interesting to me that there wasn't just a ton of blood on the floor. There wasn't blood all over the floor, or all over their legs. Their legs were very, very red, but they weren't bleeding.

As quickly as the feeling of awe came, it completely vanished, and I went back to being horrified. I was very sad for them and didn't know how to help. We were all so helpless. Eventually, my mom tried to bandage them up with some gauze that she had in the house. But nothing really changed.

~

The week after Larry and Gary were burned, Mary went on with things as usual, as if nothing had happened. Her mental state remained the same as it had always been, which might not have been good, but she didn't become crazier after burning them. There was also no sign of the remorse she initially had after burning them. She didn't change her ways. I don't know how much she and Tony talked about what she did, but he was still around a lot. They pretended everything was the same, like nothing had changed. She still locked them in the cupboard at night, and during the days, and that went on for maybe a week or two more, and then finally, she let them out. When they were finally released, they could barely walk because, by this time, gangrene had set into their legs. It was really awful.

We hadn't actually seen them for a couple of weeks because they had been locked away, so when they came upstairs, we asked them about their legs, and they said that they didn't feel a whole lot of pain anymore. I was sure it was because after all the burns and everything they had lived through, they probably just got used to it.

They were so malnourished they couldn't really do anything other than lie on their bed as we kept them company. We tried to make them laugh like we used to when things were bad. We thought that everything would soon pass and go back to normal. Then one night, Larry started to cry. He looked at his legs as if truly seeing them for the first time, and he was just really depressed and sad. At the same time, the numbness had worn off, and they were both in extreme pain. Mary came upstairs to hold Larry. She was holding him, trying to rock him to sleep. Then the earth seemed to become still. I felt as if the whole world stopped as it prepared for what was about to happen. I looked at Larry, quietly sobbing into Mary's chest, as he took his last breath and died. I could feel him die. Something in my soul cried out for him because deep down I knew what kind of loss this was. It's like we could all feel his life leave at the same time.

And at the very moment that Larry died, Gary vomited all over the floor, which was interesting, because he hadn't eaten a whole lot in a really long time. I remember thinking again how interesting it looked. How it was movie-like. Mary's child dying in her arms, and I just kept thinking how that was something you might see in a movie. I was thinking to myself that this is something that doesn't actually happen in real life, to real everyday people. It seemed so planned that she would go upstairs to hold him, and he dies in her arms, and at the same time, Gary vomits. It seemed so interesting, so staged, so dramatic.

I really didn't fully grasp the fact that I'd just witnessed my brother die. Mary started freaking out. She started shaking Larry and screaming his name. She kept saying, "Larry, Larry, wake up. Larry, come on, sweetie, wake up." She told me to run downstairs and get the Pine Sol so that she could make him smell it in hopes that it would bring him back. I went downstairs and got the Pine Sol and brought it back upstairs. We tried for what seemed like forever to bring him back. I kept looking at him, knowing that at any minute he was going to wake back up, but his body never moved.

Around this same time, Tony had come back from wherever he'd been and heard all the commotion upstairs, so he came up and saw what had happened. He, too, started freaking out, because he realized the police would have to get called and he didn't want to go to jail. Mom told him to take the rest of the money we had saved up, and the keys to the car, and she told him to drive away.

Then she told me to call the police. I called them, and they answered, but right before I could say anything, Mary told me to hang up. So, I did.

Mary had then decided that she didn't want the police to come. She told us she was going to think of another way to take care of the situation. I hung up the phone, and within a few seconds, the police had called back. I told them that it was a mistake, but the lady told me they knew where I lived, and that they were going to send someone out, so I should tell them what was wrong. I figured they were going to send someone to the house anyway, so I just told them everything. I told them what happened, that my brother was not breathing or anything like that. Within what seemed like a few minutes, the police and the ambulances were outside. All of our neighbors had come outside, and were looking at the commotion. It was a very surreal experience.

~

I remember getting rushed outside by the police officers. They then shuffled Catina, Jerry, and me into separate cop cars, dividing us up, and then questioned us individually. I wasn't saying anything. I still knew we were going to go back home and be with Mary, and I did not want to get in trouble with her for snitching. I remember one of the cops asking me what had happened, and I told him that we were all playing around with the water in the bathtub, and then Larry and Gary fell in, and since it was slick, they just couldn't get back up, and kept falling back in. And that's how they got the burns. I then told him how they pulled off their own skin. Then I told them my mom didn't take them to the hospital because she didn't want to get in trouble for something that she didn't do. The cop knew that I was lying, but I stuck with my story, because I knew we were going to go back to Mary. I just knew we were going to go back with my mom, and I was determined that I was not going to be the one that got us in trouble. Especially not now.

They finally put all three of us, Jerry, Catina, and me, in the ambulance with Gary, and we got to ride with him to the hospital. Once we got to the hospital, they took Gary somewhere else—I assume the intensive care of a burn unit. Jerry and I went to a room where they gave us physicals, and Catina went to a separate room where they gave her a physical, too. They gave us a check-up to see where we were, developmentally, as well. I was freaked out because I didn't know what was going on. No one explained anything. And so much had happened. Larry died at night between 9 and 10, I think. So here we were in the middle of the night, running around a hospital after being interrogated by cops, and after witnessing our brother die, not knowing where our mom was, not knowing what was going on. No one stayed around us long enough to tell us what was happening. Even though I was surrounded by people, I felt as if I was all alone, coming in on a play that was already in progress. But there we were in the hospital getting a physical, and we didn't know what would happen next.

They eventually took us back to the police station, and had us go to separate interrogation rooms. They told me that they had caught Tony already, and that they had arrested my mom. They told me that both of them had already told them what happened and that there was no use in me covering for them anymore. I don't know if that was a lie to get me to confess what had happened, or if it was the truth, but as I sat there, I felt that I was surrounded by cops who were going to put me in jail if I didn't tell the truth. I figured maybe since Mary had already told them, it might be okay for me to do so as well. I told them what my mom had done, what had happened. I told them everything about that night. I answered their questions.

After being at the police station for a while, we were taken to a group home of some kind. This was at like 1 or 2 o'clock in the morning. We were sitting in this place, just sitting in these chairs, doing nothing. All of the lights were out, because I'm assuming the kids were asleep, and no one was talking to us. We didn't have any contact with anyone besides each other, and we weren't really talking because we were still crying, still freaked out about everything. But there was not one time during that entire night when anyone came and just sat with us and asked us how we were; there was not one time when anyone actually wanted to take care of us. It seemed as though everyone just wanted to get the next thing done as quickly as possible.

That was deeply disturbing to me. Now I understand that after something like this happens, everyone tries to take the time to make sure that everything is done properly. They try to make sure they fill out the right forms and follow protocol. If only the powers that be had taken that same amount of care when they'd had the chance earlier, a long time ago, then maybe a life or two could have been saved.

At the time, all I could think was how stupid it all was. How obviously they didn't care about us, not even enough to tell us what was happening. How they couldn't be trusted, how Mary was right. After a while, just sitting there, a lady came and got us and took us to the Salvation Army Children's Shelter.

SHELTER

Something Beneath, Behind or Within Which a Person (Animal or Thing) Is Protected from Storms, Missiles, Adverse Conditions, etc.; Refuge

For FFY 2010, more than 3.6 million (duplicate) children were the subject of at least one report (to child protection agencies). One-fifth of these children were found to be victims with dispositions of substantiated (19.5%), indicated (1.0%), and alternative response victim (0.5%). The remaining four-fifths of the children were found to be nonvictims of maltreatment. The nonvictim dispositions with the three highest percentages are unsubstantiated (58.2%), no alleged maltreatment (9.1%) and alternative response nonvictim (8.7%)." Reports closed with no finding (1.5%) or intentionally false (0.1%), unknown (0.2%), and other (0.2%) complete the findings.[viii]

The morning news was just coming on Fox when we walked into the Salvation Army Shelter. It must have been around 5 o'clock. We were the lead story. It was so weird seeing our house, us walking out, the yellow tape, the body bag coming out and my brother being put in the ambulance. We were kind of mesmerized by it. I knew it had happened that way, but it felt almost like it was someone else on the TV. There wasn't much time to contemplate the strange world we'd entered as one of the staff members noticed that the news was on, and about us, and quickly turned the television off. But those flat images from the camera's perspective are still seared in my mind, as well as the three-dimensional ones from having lived it.

We were quickly sorted into what would become our bedrooms for the duration of our stay at the Salvation Army. Jerry and I were lucky because we got a room together with no one else in it. Catina had a room with another girl whom she had never met before. I was so exhausted at this point I pretty much collapsed into the bed. The horror, tragedy, confusion, and excitement of the night had taken their toll, and I passed out shortly after my head hit the pillow. I remember not waking up until about 3 in the afternoon, about the time the other kids in the shelter began coming home from school.

When the other kids returned, I remember a barrage of questions. Where did we come from? What happened to us? Why were we there? I don't quite remember what we told them, but I was still not quite sure myself what had happened. And I knew we weren't supposed to share family business, so I think I sort of skirted around the questions, not really answering them at all.

Trying to get used to how things ran at the shelter was difficult. While we were at home, when it wasn't awful, we had a lot of time to ourselves, a lot of autonomy. The structure, the processes, the "way we do things here" of the shelter were very different and initially a little disconcerting. But those same things became comforting, in some ways, by the time we left.

They had a very formal structure at the shelter. There was a system based on age, where younger kids were in one structure, the middle kids were in a different one, and the older kids were in yet another. The older kids got to stay up later than everyone else, the middle group of kids got to stay up a little bit longer than the younger ones who went to bed early. Each group had "age appropriate" outings, events, and rewards. I remember always wanting to be on the older kids' level, even though I was technically too young.

I quickly figured out that when I could convince the staff that I was more responsible, more mature, typically by not getting into trouble, I would be treated like the older kids. Pretty soon, I was bumped up to the older level, at least in part. I was only 10, and I think you had to be 12 or 13 to be on the level with the older kids, but I had found a way in. I was so happy and felt so lucky. I still had to go to bed at the same time as the middle-level kids, but I got to go on all of the older kids' outings.

We ended up living at the children's shelter for six months. While we were there, we had a particular caretaker named Sharon who kind of took us under her wing and became like our mom. She really seemed to want to take care of us, to be there for us, at least as much as she could. Even after we moved into the shelter, I continued to go to the same school. I think they were trying to keep things as "normal" as they could for us. Catina and Jerry didn't want to go back. Not very many, if any, of the other kids went to the same school they had been in before coming into "care."

So at school one day, in art class, I made a blue mug for Sharon with hearts and her name. I worked really hard on the mug. I wanted to show Sharon how much I appreciated her, how she cared for us, and how much she mattered. I was so excited I couldn't wait for the bus to get us back to the shelter. As soon as we got back, I gave Sharon the mug. And just as I handed the mug to Sharon, another caretaker came up and said, "Sharon, what do you say to him?" Sharon looked confused by this and said: "Thank you?" The lady looked at Sharon as if she were talking to a moronic child and replied, "No, you tell him you can't accept his gift."

Sharon looked as hurt as I was and said, "Why not?" I don't remember exactly what the lady's answer was, but basically, she told Sharon that by accepting my gift, she was allowing me to get attached to her and that was unprofessional. They wanted to make sure I didn't start to think that Sharon was going to be my next mom or something like that.

I was devastated. I was very depressed. I had put so much time into the mug. It meant so much. I really wanted to give it to her, really wanted to show her how much she mattered. And I couldn't. I shouldn't be attached to her. I shouldn't connect with her. I shouldn't care about her, and even more, she shouldn't care about me. She should be professional.

Luckily, Sharon didn't agree with the policy. Sharon quietly took the mug later that day, and snuck it into her purse, making sure none of the other staff saw that she was keeping it.

The day after we were put in the children's shelter, we went back to the hospital to see Gary. As we waited in one of the rooms, playing with some toys, I kept thinking about how great it was going to be to see him. I wanted to let him know that we had been placed somewhere that allowed us to eat more than once a day and that when he got out of the hospital, we would get to play and be with each other and not have to worry about abuse from Mary. I wasn't sure if he would be in the room with Jerry and me, but I thought there was enough space.

Then the doctor came in with a social worker, and we were told that Gary had died not too long after we left the hospital when we were taken to the children's shelter. He wasn't even there. He wasn't even alive. I went numb.

I didn't cry. I didn't talk. I didn't think. I just sat there. Silent. As I sat in that hospital, surrounded with all the toys, some door in my heart and mind shut tight. I took everything that I was feeling, everything that I was thinking and said, "That's it. I'm done. I'm done with this world. I'm done with this pain. I'm done with these people. I don't want to get close to anyone else ever again. From now on, it's just me and me only." I didn't know any other way to deal with the hurt, the disappointment, the new blows—one after another.

I didn't know how to come to terms with the fact that my life didn't look anything like it did the day before, the week before. That it would never be the same again. That it was going to be drastically different from now on. I didn't want to know how to cope with those things. I didn't know how to communicate those things. I didn't even know what I thought about those things, much less how I was supposed to feel about them. What I really wanted was to sink right there into the earth. I wanted the storms that I had admired for so long to envelop me and destroy every part of my being. I didn't want to go on in this world, to be a part of this world. I wanted to leave all the worries behind, to leave myself behind. At ten years of age, I didn't want to go on with the knowledge that I had unwillingly acquired about this frail, frightening, desperate life. I wanted to disappear.

I was so sad, so disappointed, and so drained. I just wanted it all to stop.

TRANSITION

Movement, Passage, or Change from One Position, State, Stage, Subject, Concept, etc., to Another

Four-fifths (81.3%) of victims were maltreated by a parent either acting alone or with someone else. Nearly two-fifths (37.2%) of victims were maltreated by their mother acting alone. One-fifth (19.1%) of victims were maltreated by their father acting alone. One-fifth (18.5%) of victims were maltreated by both parents. Thirteen percent of victims were maltreated by a perpetrator who was not a parent of the child. [ix]

Around the time of Larry and Gary's funeral, my biological father, Ronald Sr., came to Kansas City to try to get custody of Catina, Jerry, and me. Jerry wasn't his biological child, but he wanted to keep us together. His plan was to take us back to Indiana where he lived. But I knew my dad, and I remembered how abusive he could be. I did not want to go with him. DFS, or whoever was in charge of that kind of stuff didn't want to rush anything. I suspect they didn't want to make another mistake after the costly choices that had lost lives already. So, they did a real investigation, wanting to make sure that my dad was suitable to handle us. I think their caution was a stroke of luck for us. It slowed the process down, and we weren't packed immediately off to Indiana.

The day of the boys' funeral was quickly approaching. I learned that Mary was going to have a chance to say goodbye to Larry and

Gary at their funeral. I hoped and prayed that I would get to see her. I was convinced that we were going to go back to live with her, and I wanted to ask her how long we would have to wait until we were home with her again. I knew that Mary would explain what was going on. She would tell us what to expect. When I learned that Mary had to go to the funeral ahead of time while no one was there, I was very upset. I thought that this would be my only chance to talk to her, to get some answers, and then I found out that it wasn't going to happen. I found myself angry with everyone that stopped Mary from being with us that day. I wanted them all to feel the hurt that I was feeling at that moment. No one seemed to understand that she was our mom, my mom, their mom. How could they keep us apart?

I had never been to a funeral before. I remember getting ready for it and thinking that I didn't know how it worked. I didn't know what to expect. Ronald Sr. was there with us at the funeral. DFS thought it would be good for him to help us get through it. He walked with us throughout the day, as our support. We got there, and it seemed like a lot of people were there. I don't know if this is an accurate memory, or if it's because I was small then, but it seemed to me at the time to be a huge crowd. There were people from my school, including my teacher, and they had made little ribbons for Catina, Jerry, and me. They wanted to give them to us, so we could see that people were sympathizing with us. They wanted to let us know they were thinking about us and that they were sorry for the pain that we had to go through. A lot of kids from my school were there.

The staff, social workers, and Ronald Sr. took us into the church and told us it was a funeral, but they hadn't warned us that there were going to be open caskets. I hadn't cried since the night Larry had died and we had left Mary. As we walked through the church and down the aisle, I kept seeing people who would look at us and then start to cry. Everyone would come and say "Sorry" to us or "You poor things." And it seemed like a never-ending parade of people who wanted to apologize to us. I was so shocked by the number of people who were there that I didn't notice that I had walked right past the two caskets, and for the first ten seconds, I didn't even recognize that they were my brothers. I thought that maybe there was a double funeral going on. I didn't know how funerals worked, so I figured the caskets belonged to other people whom I didn't know and maybe these people giving me condolences mistook us for the wrong funeral somehow.

I heard Catina start to cry and saw that she was looking at the open caskets. I asked my dad who they belonged to, and he said, "Those are your brothers." And I lost it.

I couldn't stop crying. I was so horrified at what I was seeing. Their mouths were sewn together, and their eyes were sewn shut and they looked scary. I didn't know how to deal with it. I don't think I stopped crying through the entire service because I was just so horrified by how they looked. It wasn't necessarily because they were dead, it was how they looked. I think part of me thought that Larry and Gary could feel that their mouths and eyes were sewn shut, and it just freaked me out, especially because no one had prepared me for it.

I remember that during the service, I sat by my dad the entire time. I just sat close to him hoping that maybe I would get so close that I would dissolve into him and disappear. I couldn't handle the finality that the funeral entailed. I couldn't escape this pain. It seemed that the world was looking down on me, and every time I tried to get up, it threw some new twist of hurt and torment onto my shoulders. There was nowhere to go to escape the darkness that had become so encompassing. I felt that at any moment, I would realize that I, too, had died at Mary's hand. But instead of waking up in Heaven, I had gone to the never-ending torments of Hell. So, I buried myself into my dad, hoping to dissolve out of this nightmare and to wake up in a peaceful place.

That was the only time in my life that I ever remember hugging or being close to my dad. That is the only time I remember feeling we had a connection. At that moment, at the funeral, I desperately hoped that this was all an illusion, a bad dream; still, it is the only truly positive memory of my birth father.

I was so depressed and sad. I felt so lost and helpless. Helplessness had been so joined to me at the hip that it became inconceivable to ever be free of it. Finally, the funeral was over, and we got to go in a limo where we got to see a bunch of family that we hadn't see for a very long time. We met even more family we had never known. People kept coming up to us and reassuring us that everything was going to be okay. We didn't know who they were, but I think it made things a little better. They all seemed so certain. Eventually, it got easier to handle.

Since that funeral, death just hasn't affected me the same way. I've been to a few of funerals since the day of my brothers' burial, but it doesn't have anything approaching the same impact on me. I hope it's not that I'm a cold person, a person who doesn't have any feelings in regard to other peoples' lives. I just think that after seeing something like that, something so traumatic while I was so young, there's just not much that can shake me up the same way.

Not that I would like to see anything top it, but there isn't much that would shake me to the core like seeing the bodies of two of my brothers. It's something that kind of worries me. It makes me wonder if having that kind of detachment from death is good for me. Is that something that is okay to feel—especially this long afterwards? Even to this day, death, to me, is just death. Yes, I have experienced the general sadness of losing a person, but I don't know if it hits me the way that it's supposed to. I don't know if I will ever have as strong a feeling as I had at my brothers' funeral. I think that my mind or my heart has blocked itself from feeling that kind of pain and despair again. I'm not sure it's something that I ever want to feel again. So, while part of me thinks I should work on "fixing" this piece of myself, the other part of me says leave well enough alone.

CONFUSION

Disorder; Upheaval; Tumult; Chaos

The number of reported child fatalities due to child abuse and neglect has fluctuated during the past 5 years. A national estimated 1,560 children (compared with 1,750 children for FFY 2009) died from abuse and neglect. The national fatality rate per 100,000 children in the population was 2.07 for FFY 2010 compared with a national fatality rate of 2.32 for FFY 2009.[x]

In the days following the deaths of Larry and Gary, I felt a lot of new emotions, one of which was betrayal. When we were first taken away from Mary, I found that I was angry with her, not because of the trauma that she had put my siblings and me through, but because she had left us. I was so angry with her that she let the police take us and put us with people that we didn't know. I kept asking myself how a mother could do this to her kids. How could she allow some random strangers to take her children away from her without a fight? I was hurt that after everything we were put through, this was the fate that we were destined for. It's hard to believe, but I was actually angry that we were taken away from Mary. I didn't want some new family with new rules. I figured that with my luck, I would end up in another abusive family that didn't care about me. At least with Mary, I knew the routine, and I knew that deep down she did care about me and love me.

There were a lot of back-and-forth feelings like that for me. One day I would be extremely happy that I was finally in a place where I didn't have to worry about being starved or beaten for being too loud. The next day, I'd be overwhelmingly depressed when I woke up expecting to see Larry and Gary, and, upon realizing they were dead, I would look for comfort from the person that murdered them. I couldn't get my emotions in check. I was missing the person who destroyed my life; I longed to talk to her, to hug her, to tell her that I loved her. I should have just hated her, just kept wishing her dead, but I couldn't. Was I so brainwashed that I missed the abuse? It was as if there was a cloud of darkness growing in me. I tried not to let it show to others, but on the inside, I was crumbling—and quickly. I found that the best way to suppress those feelings was to keep myself busy hanging out with other people and not allowing myself time alone to think. Then night would come, and I would have to lie in bed with only my thoughts, and the storm would come back and hover until I fell asleep angry with myself and with the world.

When I eventually went back to school, I remember feeling as though everyone around me knew my story. As I walked into the front doors of the school, I saw a table set up that was hosting a fundraiser. I stood frozen as I realized that the fundraiser was for me and my siblings. I hadn't realized that I was going to a school where so many people cared about my well-being and the well-being of my family. It was quite humbling, but at the same time, I was embarrassed. I knew other people weren't supposed to be in our family business.

People were coming up and apologizing and being extra nice and sensitive toward me. At first, it was nice, and I enjoyed the attention, but I soon realized the drawbacks of people knowing about the most sensitive part of my life. There was this girl in my class named Ashley, who was overweight for her age and not very nice to people. After a couple of weeks of me being back in school, Ashley felt that it was okay to make jokes about what had happened to my brothers. She would say things like, "You know what I'm going to do when I have children? If my kids are bad, I'm gonna dump them in hot water and kill them. Oh, you know what that's like, Ronald, don't you?" I hated her. I wanted every bad thing that could possibly happen to her to happen. I wanted her to know the true meaning of pain. She was the exception, however. For the most part, everyone was very understanding and tried to behave in a caring and protective manner.

I remember feeling so depressed and sad that we had to spend Thanksgiving and Christmas at the Children's Shelter with all of the other kids who had no families. Our first holiday with half of the family missing was so depressing it was nearly unbearable. It was our first Christmas without our mom. I had really hoped that we would be back at home for the holiday season. That was the only gift I truly wanted. The upside, however, with being in the shelter for the holidays was that we knew we were going to have a meal on both Thanksgiving and Christmas. As I prepared for spending the holidays at the shelter, I was reminded of one Christmas with Mary where our Christmas dinner consisted of us sitting on the floor with a ham and a bucket of popcorn—you know the kind you can buy around the holidays. It was still a fun and happy time. We had watched old Michael Jackson music videos and listened to oldies music, which was a family tradition when we were hanging out together. It was just a really good time. We were dancing and everything. And even though we didn't have much, knowing that we had each other was enough. We didn't get presents or anything, but it didn't really matter to us because we didn't know anything else anyway, so it wasn't a big deal.

One of the things that I was most thankful for after being taken away from Mary was how hard DFS worked to keep Catina, Jerry, and me together. I knew that most kids didn't get to stay with their brothers and sisters when they were put into foster care, and I felt very blessed that we did. It was a great feeling knowing that we were still going to be together. Even when we eventually moved to our foster home in Belton, we got to stay together.

When I was at the children's shelter, I got to experience my first kiss with a girl who I won't name to save her from embarrassment.

She was 13, and I was 10 at the time. And, even though we weren't supposed to have boyfriends and girlfriends at the Children's Shelter, we didn't care. We still liked each other, and we decided we wanted to try to be secret boyfriend and girlfriend, and I remember writing her a letter telling her that I liked her. I tried to sneak it to her, but one of the caretakers found it and decided that she wanted to read it to the rest of the caretakers. And I remember them laughing at me. And calling me a little pimp, and things like that, and just teasing me. They tried to get the kids who stayed at the children's shelter not to be there more than six months without finding a placement for them. Well, my secret girlfriend, hereafter known as SG, had been there longer than that, so they finally had to find another place for her. I thought she was going to a family, so the night before she left, Sharon told me that if I wanted to, I could kiss SG goodbye. I had been bragging about knowing what I was doing, even though I had no clue at all. I got so excited that I ran to my room and got my toothbrush and toothpaste and ran to the bathroom and brushed my teeth three times. I brushed my tongue and everything because I wanted my breath to be super fresh and perfect. Some older kids showed up to see how I'd do. I remember going for it and having no clue how to kiss or anything like that. Then as she went in to kiss me, I remember opening my mouth and pretty much swallowing her.

As I think back on it, I must have looked like I was trying to engulf her head into my mouth. It was the most awkward experience, and I was practically licking her because I thought that was what you were supposed to do. When we took a little break, she whispered in my ear, "Don't use your tongue like that. Just keep your mouth closed." At the time I thought, "Oh, I don't care, because I was doing the coolest thing ever," but when I think about it now, I'm just so embarrassed because I can't believe I did something like that and that I was so awful at it.

I remember Jerry being so angry because I got to kiss a girl and he didn't. SG tried to make it up to him by giving him a kiss on the cheek. I was so angry with him after that, because he tried to experience something that was supposed to be my happy moment. He was trying to take away something that I would get to brag about. It's funny how upset I was even though his kiss was on the cheek and wasn't any big deal. It was my first kiss ever, and it's one of those memories that I hope I always keep. It's a great story, even if there was rather poor execution. It will always be funny to me.

As I mentioned earlier, when we moved to the Children's Shelter, my biological father, Ronald Sr., tried to get custody of Catina, Jerry, and me. I remember playing basketball on the court at the shelter during one of his visits. At one point in the game, he asked me to do something, and I didn't want to do it. Shannon, who was like our therapist/social worker at the shelter, wasn't paying attention at the time. I remember him getting really close to my face. He gave me that same death glare that I had seen too many times before from Mary, and he said, "I can't wait to get you home." I knew that he meant that he was going to beat me for disobeying him. It scared the hell out of me. It made it suddenly real that I might actually end up living with him. That really scared me; I knew how terrible it would be. I didn't tell anyone. I don't even think that I told Shannon what he said, even though it scared me so badly.

Not too long after arriving at the Children's Shelter, I went and got a physical, and I found out that I had a hernia, and that I'd have to have surgery for it. Shannon stayed with me in the hospital that night after the surgery. She slept in a chair at the foot of the bed. It was comforting knowing that I wasn't there alone. I remember watching *Sabrina the Teenage Witch* on TV at like one in the morning. It was like having my mom with me, taking care of me. The next morning, Catina and SG called me before they headed off to school to wish me to get better. I was very thrilled and relieved when I got to go home later that day. It was nice to get all the hugs from people welcoming me back to the shelter, nice to feel wanted and cared for. It was beginning to feel like home.

FOSTER

To Promote the Growth or Development of; Further; Encourage; to Care for or Cherish

Ronald Sr. and his wife were denied custody due to past histories and ongoing challenges. One day, we were told that Jerry, Catina, and I were moving to Belton, Missouri, because DFS had found us a foster home. I remember being very confused. First, I had no idea where Belton was. Second, I couldn't understand why they were sending us to live with someone else when we were going back to Mary soon. "Shouldn't we just stay here in the shelter until we are able to go home?" I was worried that Mary wouldn't be able to find us if we were with another family.

It still hadn't dawned on me that I was never going to see my mother again. It wasn't until after I learned, while living with Jack and Kaylee, that Mary was going to spend the rest of her life in jail that it truly hit me. The moment I called the police was the moment that I said goodbye to my mother. When this realization hit me, I felt an overwhelming guilt.

"If I had done something differently, she would be free right now. If I hadn't called, we'd be home with her. If I'd said something different, she'd be free." The thoughts swarmed in my mind constantly. It was my fault that Mary was going to jail for the rest of her life. I should have been more of a man. I should have protected my family. I should have protected Mary. It was my job to take care of the family and make sure everything was okay. I had failed. I had just as much cause to be in jail as Mary did.

Even today, there is a little of that guilt left. I don't think it's something that will ever leave me. Of course, I know now, cognitively, that it wasn't my fault, and I know that there really isn't a whole lot that I could have done, but I still feel that guilt.

So, after six months in the Children's Shelter, Catina, Jerry, and I were moved in with Jack and Kaylee. Jack and Kaylee were an older married foster-care couple who lived in Belton, Missouri. I remember telling the social worker at the time that I wanted a family that was rich. I wanted a family that had a big house and the ability to give me all the things that I wanted. I remember thinking, as I arrived at their farm, that Jack and Kaylee could definitely do that.

It wasn't like I became a millionaire and got everything I wanted. But the fact that they could provide not only food and utilities but also toys and clothes for me made adjusting to life with them a little bit easier. But I wasn't prepared to let anyone else into my life. They would just have to accept that. I had decided after my life with Mary that I just wasn't going to do it again. I didn't want to open myself up to the possibility of someone else letting me down hard.

Jack and Kaylee were very different people than Mary. They were very sensitive, ultra-sensitive, about almost everything. I don't mean that they were sensitive about how they felt, but about how we felt, and how things affected us. I think we really needed this after Mary, but it was so completely different. I was so skittish, so scared, very scared. If someone yelled, it startled me. Sometimes I would cry, and sometimes I would get angry because yelling of any kind, or excitement, or anything out of the ordinary would scare me. If someone would jokingly tap me or jokingly hit me, I would start crying because it would scare me so much.

Right after we moved in with Jack and Kaylee, we started going to therapy, which at first, I thought was totally stupid. I didn't think I needed therapy. I didn't want to talk to anyone. I told myself that I had everything under control.

I already knew what I was going to do: I was not going to let anyone in. I had already figured it out. I didn't need any help figuring that out with the help of some therapists who were ultimately just looking for their next paycheck.

Then I met Helen Wiser.

HELP

To Make Easier or Less Difficult; Contribute to; Facilitate

The age of a child greatly affects where he or she is likely to be placed when in foster care. In general, younger children are more likely to be living with families and older children more likely to be in group homes or institutions. For example, 33 percent of children ages one to five are placed with relatives compared with only 11 percent of those 16 and older. Only one percent of children ages one to five are living in group homes or institutions compared with 36 percent of those 16 and older. Unfortunately, these older youth in group and institutional care are more likely to exit foster care when they reach the age of majority without the benefit of the family connections more easily developed in a family-based setting.[xi]

Helen Wiser was the owner of Midtown Psychological in Kansas City while we were in care. Helen became my therapist, and it seemed to me that she actually cared. She stuck around. Every time we met, she would try to get me to open up more and more. But it wasn't just by asking questions; it was by having me play games. Through the games, she'd get me talking about things. Something that happened in the game, that had to do with the game—but also that had to do with my old life. Slowly, painfully, I began to open up.

Around the same time, at least as I remember it, I was also sent to a psychiatrist who prescribed me Risperdal, which was an anger medication, and Zoloft, which was an anti-depressant. I remember being so angry that I was put on medication. I thought that I was fine. I didn't need any medication. I didn't think I had a problem with anger, a problem with depression. I thought that medication was only for people who lived in "crazy homes." I didn't need medication. I was going to show them. I was fine. Unfortunately, I decided the best way to show them was by acting out. So the medicine seemed even more necessary. Everything I tried to do to show them how strong I was signaled that I was in desperate need of help. I ended up verifying for them that I needed to be put on something to help balance out my moods. As much as I disliked, and still do the idea of medication, I suspect, as an adult, that the meds may have played a positive role in making the therapy more successful.

As time passed, I got closer and closer to Helen and opened up a lot more. I started to try to move towards a healthier version of myself, a view that I had in my mind but may not have been the same on the outside. I was looking for a "me" I could be more comfortable with. It seemed to me that Helen and I were partners in trying to find the real me, bring the real me back. I really trusted her. I believed she was trying to do what was right for me, not just serving her own self-interest.

Then one day, Helen told me that she couldn't be my therapist anymore. Someone else was going to be my new therapist, was taking over my case.

"See! See!" I screamed to myself in my mind. "What were you thinking? You know you can't trust anyone! This is a prime example of why I don't want to let people into my life, because I open up to people, and I put my heart out there and try to show them who I am, and they just leave me. It's all an act. They don't really care!"

I began acting out again. In the extreme. I started doing whatever I could to draw attention to myself, almost exclusively in a negative way. I would show them all. I would make them pay attention to me, even if it was in a negative way. I would find a way to get the attention I wanted.

There was nothing wrong with the therapist who replaced Helen, but I would have nothing to do with her. Eventually, Helen did become my therapist again. I felt that I had won the battle to get what I wanted. As an adult, I also see that was the first time I consciously manipulated the system to get my needs met.

Shortly after starting individual therapy with Helen, we also started doing family therapy—Jerry, Catina, and I. I tried to make it as much of a joke as possible. I didn't want to talk about my feelings in front of Jerry and Catina. I didn't want them laughing at me or thinking that I was weak. There were lots of times when I just tried to make it into a game.

TEST

The Means by Which the Presence, Quality or Genuine Nature of Anything Is Determined; a Means of Trial

> The Children's Bureau reports a decline in children in foster care or being adopted in the United States for the year of 2011 to 401,000 children, down from 406,000 from 2010.[xii]

Over the next two years with Jack and Kaylee, I felt that I was settling in. I began to grow a bit more. I began to learn more things, do more things. One of my proudest accomplishments was learning how to swim. I don't know if anyone I grew up with could swim. There wasn't a lot of opportunity for swimming lessons. No one had pools in their back yards, at least not ones more than a foot deep. It wasn't easy. I had to really work at it, but when I made it the whole length of the pool for the first time, I felt as though I'd really tackled something. I went to a school and actually made friends. I even actually started to try to make decent grades. I did my schoolwork as though it mattered, at least a little.

When I was in seventh grade, I got picked to be Scrooge in the little play that we put on for my English class. I loved it. That was the first time that I thought about becoming an actor. It really sparked my interest. Ever since that performance, hearing all the people laugh at the right moments and seeing their captivated faces, I knew that acting was something that I wanted to do. That it was something I was good at. That I enjoyed.

There was a point in time when Jack and Kaylee decided that I had stabilized. They decided to take me off my medication, to see how I'd do without it. For a couple of weeks, I was fine. Then I started getting into trouble. What I considered horse-play and being a normal pre-teen boy, they (the powers that be—teachers, volunteers, etc.) considered distress signals. I got in trouble at school for playing a prank on one of the college-aged summer volunteers we had. She was a girl just helping out for the summer program. I didn't really have an opinion about her, didn't particularly like or dislike her. A couple of the other volunteers, guys, dared me to pour water on her. So I did it. She was furious. She started to drag me down to the principal's office to write me up for the prank. The guys ran after her and explained to her that they had told me to dump the water on her. She let me go and started yelling at the guys, telling them how it wasn't funny and that her clothes were ruined. Actually, I thought that it was pretty funny.

When I got home, I told Jack and Kaylee about my day, including the close trip to the office, and they were very upset and thought that this was me going back to being angry and acting out. They started thinking that maybe it wasn't such a good idea to take me off my medication so quickly. I knew I was stupid for telling them. That was all I needed. Then I got in trouble again. Jerry and I were swimming and were roughhousing in the pool. We took turns wrestling and dunking each other under the water. Well, one time when I dunked him, he started choking. Soon, what was just horseplay to me turned into an attempt on my brother's life to Jack and Kaylee.

After this incident, Jack and Kay were sure that taking me off my medication was a bad idea. They took me to Crittenton, a psychiatric hospital, and had me stay there while the psychiatrists tried to figure out what was wrong with me, and what the best medications for me would be. After a few days in the psychiatric facility, the staff realized there was nothing dramatically wrong, and they let me go. I remember thinking how everyone was so dumb.

They were overprotective and way too jittery. Obviously, it was their problem. It wasn't mine.

During my short stay at Crittenton, as I waited in a lunch line, I bumped into a girl in front of me. As she turned around, I was so stunned I almost dropped my plate. She was my secret girlfriend from the Children's Shelter. She wasn't there for a short stay. In my mind, until that moment, I had believed that she went to a nice home somewhere with nice parents when she left the shelter. It was so depressing.

Then it hit me how strange it was that we even saw each other at all, especially when I was only there for a few days, and there were multiple lunch shifts. What were the odds? That place was so huge that we could have easily gone the whole time without seeing each other.

We got to talk for a few minutes, and mostly, it was awkward. I felt sad for her. I still do. I don't know if she ever found a forever home or if she ended up like so many other kids that have to age out of the system without ever having a family. I don't know if anyone was ever able to take care of her.

While I was in Crittenton for only a few days, it felt like an eternity. I remember I thought each day there was the longest day of my life. I felt that I had been there for years. They had put me on so much Risperdal that I was sleepy all the time, and I couldn't do anything. I felt so tired and drained just keeping my head up. Sitting down was all that I could do. They would let us go to the gym and have a sort of "free time" once a day. I would go in there, and all the kids would be playing, and I would just sit at the wall. I wouldn't do anything because I had no energy to move. Luckily, I had my own room, because there weren't a lot of kids in my ward. I remember getting visits from Jack and Kaylee and from my therapists and different people, and I just wished that they didn't have to leave because after they were gone, the time would just go by so slowly. I didn't think I was going to make it. I thought I was going to have to be there for a very long time. I thank God that I ended up not having to be there very long at all.

BREAK

To Smash, Split or Divide into Parts Violently; Reduce to Pieces or Fragments

There were times while in therapy when I thought I would play games with the therapists. They would constantly ask me to talk to them about Mary and let some feelings out about her. I never wanted to. I was fine. It wasn't any of their business. They were dumb for trying to pry something out of me that wasn't going to come out. Once, during a family therapy session, the therapists were trying to get Catina, Jerry, and me to talk about Mary around each other, and though Catina and Jerry were opening up, I wasn't budging. Well, after what the therapists' considered a breakthrough, they allowed Catina and Jerry to leave but kept me in the room with them. They kept telling me that I needed to talk about Mary and that they weren't going to let me go until did. I figured that since they were being so persistent, I would play a little game with them.

I figured that if they wanted to see if I was truly crazy, then I would show them some crazy in hopes that they would get freaked out and leave me alone. So I started pretending like Mary was talking through me, that I was possessed by her, and that she was talking about how she couldn't let me go and how she couldn't let me be happy, and she was scared that I would be mistreated, etc. Before I knew it, I wasn't pretending anymore. I mean, I wasn't possessed or anything, but I was allowing myself to talk as if someone else were saying the things that I was too embarrassed to say were coming from me. They were all my fears that I had pent up inside me. All the fears of letting someone else into my life, fears of letting go of Mary, fears that I was going back to her, and it was going to be worse.

And I remember breaking from my breakdown and looking at Helen's face, and she shot one of the therapists a look of just "Wow." It wasn't necessarily that this kid is crazy, but "Oh, wow, this kid has a lot of things that have built up in him that he's finally letting out." I was going nuts. I was running around the room and knocking things over and screaming at the therapists that they couldn't have me because I was Mary, and she wasn't going to let them have me. I told them that they weren't talking to Ron but to Mary. So they started talking to Mary and telling her that it was okay to let the boy go, that they would take care of him, that she had to let him go.

Afterwards, I just thought it was so cool. I was crying and everything, and got all these emotions out that had built up over time. They didn't write me off and say, "You're nuts. Stop trying to get attention by being her." And they didn't try to talk to me and say, "Ronald, snap out of this. Ronald, don't be dumb." They were like, "Mary, we'll take care of him. Mary, you can let him go. Mary, he's safe."

I think that was the beginning of my letting her go and of me letting go of that part of my life. As I look back, that's about when I started moving in a direction where I could get help, where I could be healthy, where I could have a future. It was a good feeling.

We had a lot of people supporting us when we were in foster care, far more than most kids in the system have. It's interesting to look at which ones you remember and which you don't. It's not logical; it's not rational. There were some people that I remember in detail who were only there for a short period of time, and others who were around a lot, for a long time, who I have no memory of at all. In fact, I've denied they existed, only to be proven wrong. But for whatever reason, a few stick out. There was a woman named Pazia who worked at Midtown where we went for therapy. She used to come out to the farm and would work as our nanny, for lack of a better term. I remember thinking that she was the greatest. She was so cool and nice to us and so soft-spoken. She would always try to make us happy, and she always seemed like she genuinely wanted the best for us. There was one time when we were outside playing, and Jerry and I got into a fight over nothing. He was yelling at me, and I was saying, "Yeah, go ahead. Yeah. Get it out. Don't let anyone walk all over you. Don't let anyone push you around. Get it out. You stand up for yourself." I don't want to say I was patronizing him, but I guess that's what I was doing. Anyway, Pazia came over and calmly made us stop, and before we knew it, we weren't fighting anymore, and we didn't even realize we had stopped fighting. She was a really, really nice lady.

Our DFS worker was a lady named Angie. The first time I met Angie was at the children's shelter. At the time she wasn't my DFS worker. She was this other girl's DFS worker, and my first interaction with her was when I was chasing this girl around the room. One of the rules at the shelter was that guys were not allowed in girls' rooms, and girls were not allowed in guys' rooms. Well, I was chasing this girl, and she ran to her room, and I stepped in there, and quickly stepped back out but not before someone asked, "Hey, were you just in her room?" I tried to lie, and I said no. Well, Angie had been sitting there with the girl she was working with, and she said, "Yeah. He was in that room," and I got in trouble. I remember thinking, "That lady is such a bitch. I hate her. I hope I never see her again." Then when we moved in with Jack and Kaylee, she became our DFS worker. I quickly learned that she was a really nice, really cool person. She used to take us around places in her Jaguar. She took us to get our pictures and put them on the website for us, so that we could be adopted by a family and things like that. She definitely made up for the lack of care in social work that we used to have while living with Mary, and she helped me to begin to have less harsh feelings towards "the system."

Katie, who was Helen's daughter, worked at Midtown as well, and she was kind of like our mentor, and she would take us out to places, and she was just really nice to us. She would let us spend the night at her house. We used to go to Helen's house during the summer and swim in her pool. And we'd go out to Helen's neighborhood during Halloween and trick or treat, and Katie was always there and always taking care of us. I remember one time when Katie and I were joking around, and she was driving us to Helen's house, and she said something, and I said something back. Then she gave me like a joking punch on the arm, and it triggered something in me, and I remember just crying. Of course, it took her by surprise, and she began to worry what was wrong with me. She kept asking why I was crying, and I said it was because of her hitting me. She just felt so awful, because she didn't want me to feel scared of her, but in that moment, I was. There's this phase you go through. It doesn't make sense, not even inside your own head. But some little thing will just slam you right back into the midst of whatever bad stuff was in your past. A little thing will trigger this big response. That was one of those times. Katie is one of those people who would never intentionally hurt anyone, but it just scared me, and I didn't know how to react except to cry.

One the happiest times at the beginning of our stay with Jack and Kaylee was Christmas Day when we received our Red Bags from the Division of Family Services, (DFS). It was so cool because we got these giant red trash bags filled with Christmas presents just for us. You've got to remember Christmas really didn't happen at our house. The Christmas when we were living at the shelter, we got presents, but not like this. Jerry, Catina, and I each got our own bag. We didn't have to share. I will always remember the red bags from Jack and Kaylee's house. What made it even better was that we still got the presents that Jack and Kaylee had bought for us as well as presents from other people. I finally understood, on a shallow level, why Christmas was such a big deal. It felt so great having actual presents on Christmas, and having an actual Christmas dinner, and having actual birthday parties and presents and things like that. Normalcies such as those helped immensely in allowing us to adjust to living without Mary. It made leaving her in the past a whole lot easier. Later, the true meaning of Christmas would take more prominence in my life, but at that point, I was just finally figuring out what was good about being a kid.

Our first time being able to trick-or-treat was also while living with Jack and Kaylee. When we lived at the children's shelter, we were there for Halloween, but we kids were not allowed to go outside unless we were on a supervised field trip. So what we really had to do was to go just right outside the door of the shelter and have people drop candy into our bags, but we couldn't go to houses or anything like that. So it was a very fun experience with Jack and Kay. I got to have my first real store-bought costume and my first trick-or-treat bag. I got to go to actual houses and say, "Trick or Treat." Even though I was eleven the first time I got to trick-or-treating, I was so happy, and I didn't care. I was so caught up in the fact that I was doing something that I never thought I'd get to do in my life. I got to be with my friends and go around and get scared and scare people with my costume and dress up—not to mention the candy. It was absolutely amazing!

At some point in the therapy process, the therapists thought that it would be a good idea to have our grandparents come to a session, so we could ask them questions about why Mary was the way she was. We asked them if our mom was beaten when she was young, because we thought that might explain why she had done what she did to us. They said that she got spanked the least out of all their kids, as they just couldn't bring themselves to spank her because she was the youngest. They said that they didn't know what happened to her, and they said that when she turned seventeen or eighteen, she ran away from home and came back engaged to Ronald Sr. It was the first time they'd seen her in a long while. Then they told us about how my mom got married, and life progressed as it did.

I was already pretty cynical. It was hard to know what to believe from them. I didn't know if they might have been trying to make it seem like it wasn't an issue so that they didn't seem at fault at all. I don't really know what the true story is. I guess I never will. But I tried to make sense of it. I could see it being plausible that she might have just not been right in the head. That felt better than the thought that they had turned her into a monster, or that they hadn't done enough to save us. Maybe it was easier to just accept that she was somehow off-balance. If it were truly an isolated incident, that might mean there was hope that I wouldn't turn out to be just as crazy.

NORMAL

Conforming to the Standard or the Common Type; Usual; Not Abnormal

When I started school in Belton, I was very afraid of what it was going to be like. It was my first time in a new school. Prior to that, I had been at Faxon Montessori, so all of my friends had been with me pretty much my entire school-aged life. Now, I was going to have to make new friends. I didn't really know how to do that. I'm not sure that anyone can teach you how to do that. How to make friends—it's kind of trial and error.

As time passed, I did acquire a good group of friends. That really helped with my adjustment to my new life. It wasn't long before most of the people at my school knew that I was a foster kid. It was kind of obvious. They used to ask me all the time why I lived with two white people. I would just tell them, "Because my mom can't take care of me anymore." For the most part, that would usually be a sufficient answer. It was nice that everyone knew I was a foster kid, even if they didn't know why, or even if they really didn't know what that was. It took some of the pressure off me. I didn't feel that I had to go to school hiding a huge secret every day, which was a nice change. After a while in Belton, school became normal for me. I had friends like normal kids, and I had all of the problems that normal kids in middle school have. From homework to girls, I blended in with everyone else in school, and I never had to hear anyone say that I was abnormal because of my life or because I was in foster care. I just fit in.

Going to school in Belton was also really nice because it gave me a fresh start. A fresh, new school with a new outlook on life was just what I needed at that point. I got to make new friends who didn't know the details of my past. They didn't feel sorry for me, they didn't taunt me, and they didn't judge me based on what they heard or saw on the news.

At the same time, being with Jack and Kaylee was hard, too. The most obvious reason was that they were a white family. I had never been in a situation where I was being taken care of and provided for by white people. I found that people at my school quickly adjusted to that and didn't see me in any weird kind of way or treat me any differently, even when they knew my foster parents were white. But at first, it felt really strange to me. It just didn't naturally make sense. You certainly couldn't hide it.

Jerry adjusted the best to having a white family; it seemed to me. I'm sure his being biracial didn't hurt. It took me a bit longer. I think of all of us, Catina seemed to have the most problems adjusting. She really wanted to be in a black family; particularly, she wanted a black mom. She had a hard time letting go of the past and embracing the possibility of a new future.

One day after school, I went over to a friend's house to hang out. I had gotten permission to ride the bus home with him. As we were waiting to get to his stop, I decided to tell him why I was in foster care. I don't know why I chose that moment or that boy, but I did. I told him about how my brothers used to get fed dog food, and how we had been beaten on a pretty regular basis. After a couple moments of silence, he told me that he too was fed dog food by his birth parents and that was one of the reasons why he was adopted.

I remember getting angry at him. I couldn't believe that it was coincidence that my closest friend would have gone through the same thing as me. I figured he had to be lying. I said to him, "You don't have to lie to try to make me feel better or whatever it is you are trying to do. You shouldn't say stuff like that if it isn't true." He looked taken aback and told me that he was serious and that it was a serious issue in his life that he had to deal with. But he never had anyone he could actually talk to about it. I apologized to him, but even to this day, I wonder if he was telling the truth or if he was just trying to make me feel like I wasn't an outcast. Sometimes the doubt and cynicism doesn't go away. Things just weren't often what they seemed in my early life. I'm never really sure if they are even now.

TRIAL

A Tentative or Experimental Action in Order to Ascertain Results or

the Examination before a Judicial Tribunal of the Facts Put in Issue in a Cause, Often Includes Issues of Law as Well as Those of Facts

While living with Jack and Kaylee, Mary's court trial finally was scheduled. It was supposed to be highly publicized due to the horrific nature of the charges against her. Our therapists, at that time, along with Jack and Kay thought it would be a good idea if we weren't around for the trial. They decided to take us to Florida for the week of the trial in hopes that we would miss the worst of it.

We got all of our assignments from our teachers, and took our school things with us and went down to Florida to stay with Kaylee's brother for the week. It was our first trip to Florida, obviously, and it was really the first vacation (that was a real vacation) we ever took. We got to go to the beach and got to see whales—we even saw a dolphin swim by us when we were in the ocean—and we collected bags and bags of seashells. During the day, we'd do our schoolwork and take breaks by going and jumping into the swimming pool. That pool was so amazing because, at night, the lights in it would make it change colors. We would want to spend all night swimming in the different colors of the pool. It was an amazingly fun experience. And not once did I think that getting to eat was the best part of being on vacation, though that was good too.

It really did take my mind off everything – off my mom and off the things that came along with thinking about the trial. It helped me feel like a normal kid. It wasn't until recently that I understood it took quite a lot to get permission for us to go. The prosecution really wanted us to testify at the trial. To face Mary in court and say what she had done. I think I remember having to talk to the judge a time or two, but that would have been impossible for me at that time. I still haven't confronted Mary about what she did; I certainly couldn't have at that age.

Mary was sentenced to eight consecutive life sentences without the possibility of parole. I wasn't quite sure how I felt when I first learned about this. On one hand, I was very angry with her for all that she had put us through and the fact that she had murdered two of my brothers, but on the other hand, she was my mom. Even after everything, she was still my mom. I felt a deep allegiance—loyalty— toward her. It was still my job to protect her. There was a point in time when I told myself that one day, I would go and try to have my mother freed. I would just need to get a bit older, and then I could have her sentence overturned. She had to be mentally unstable and therefore shouldn't be held entirely responsible for the deaths of Gary and Larry. I felt it was up to me to go before the courts and fight for my mother and give her a second chance. I felt that DFS was just as responsible for what had happened to us as Mary. I felt that if they had done their job better, they could have prevented the deaths of my two brothers, and they could have forced Mary to get the help that she needed. Then she would have been able to take care of us and be a good mother.

I don't really know how I feel about that today. I find that I have some of the same conflicts that I did almost ten years ago. Part of me thinks that she should remain in jail, but there is also a part that tells me it's up to me to help her and find her the treatment she needs. I don't know if Mary should be free, but I do think that she at least deserves to be somewhere that can deal with her mental disabilities. *(Note: Mary did try to use a multiple personality defense in her trial, and while I strongly believe Mary has mental/emotional issues, I do not believe she has multiple personality disorder. I also believe that while she may not have known what she was doing at particular moments, she did know that what she put us through was evil. She understood that we weren't safe, and she knew it was her job as our mother to keep us safe.)*

Tony was also sentenced to some jail time but not as much as Mary. I believe that there was even a possibility of parole for him. When I learned about this, I remember being very angry that he got a better deal than Mary. It was as much his fault as hers in my mind. Things were always better when she was alone and would change for the worse whenever she was with a guy. I felt that was especially true with Tony. I always blamed the men in my mother's life for her craziness, and Tony was not innocent himself. He beat us, he starved us, and he was part of Larry and Gary's deaths, too.

I found that I had more hatred for him than I did for Mary. I remember that when I first heard that Tony might be out one day, I told myself I would fight it. If that meant speaking at his parole hearing, I would. I felt that if I had to hire a lawyer to fight his appeal, then that is what I would do. I wanted to do everything in my power to make sure he never walked free again. I felt that if Mary could never go free, then he shouldn't, either.

The longer we lived with Jack and Kaylee, the more people I connected to. Billie was one of those people. She was Jack and Kaylee's adopted son's girlfriend, who remained part of the family even after the dating stopped. My adjustment to Billie was probably the quickest out of everyone that I opened up to while living with Jack and Kaylee. Billie helped me to fit in and not feel like everything that happened was the end of the world. It was nice to have someone who was old enough to take me places and look after me, but not so old that I felt that I couldn't tell her anything. Billie made me feel that she was always going to be there to look out for me, like a big sister. Even though Catina was my biological older sister, I was always the one that had to take care of her, so I wasn't used to relying on her for protection, for insight, for advice. Maybe that was why I adjusted to Billie so quickly. She made me feel normal because she was like an older sister I didn't have to take care of, but one who would take care of me, instead. This one thing that might not seem very important was actually a life-changer for me. It allowed me for the first time to feel as if I didn't always have to be in "adult mode." I felt that I could let myself be taken care of without feeling that without my protection, Jerry and Catina would be in danger.

The therapists who worked with my family were so much a part of my life that they became like family themselves. I was able to talk to them about anything, and they were always just a phone call away if I needed something. It was nice knowing that I always had someone there who would help me with my problems, no matter how small or dumb they might have seemed. I don't know how my life would have turned out if I didn't have all of those people in my life while in Belton. A lot of the breakthroughs that changed my life happened in that safe and protected space on a farm in Belton, Missouri. And without that space, care, time, and patience, I'm not sure I would have survived the transition to a different family than Mary's. That time, that space, and those people, were essential to my survival.

One of the things that first unnerved me, but later inspired me, was everyone telling me that I was smart, and that I could do anything that I wanted in life and be anything that I wanted to be. It was my first time ever hearing those words being said to me. At first, it was hard for me to hear, and I thought everyone was lying to me. I felt that I couldn't be all that smart since I didn't tell anyone what was happening to me when I lived with Mary. How could I be smart if I let Larry and Gary die? I thought everyone was just saying that, so they could get me to do what they wanted me to. But everyone kept saying it and encouraging me to try my hardest, so that I could show everyone just how bright I was.

In time, people saying that to me inspired in me the greatest feeling in the world because it made me feel as if I was worth something, and that I actually had a place in the world. I started to feel like I *was* smart, and it made me want to prove to people that I was. My favorite way to do so was through psychology. I loved trying to figure people out, and still do to this day; it's a real accomplishment for me to figure out not only what's wrong with people, but how I can help. I feel that I have a special talent for figuring people out in that way. I think it's one of the reasons that I was often in Mary's good graces, which, in turn, helped me to survive. But I didn't figure out that this was a unique sort of ability until moving to Belton.

I'm afraid, however, that my skills weren't always used for good. In my early days in Belton, I would often use them to get people upset. I knew the exact things to say or not say that would make people angry. But after a while, I started to want to help people and often found myself being the person that people would come to at school with their problems because I was not only good at listening, but I was also good at telling people ways they could deal with their problems and helping them to feel that they were not alone. People were now regularly telling me that I was worth something and that I had potential. It made a real difference in my life that this was coming from important people, grown-up people. I began to feel that I could live in Belton forever. I began to feel that I had a life, a future, a place. My place.

DISRUPT

To Cause Disorder or Turmoil in; to Destroy, Usually Temporarily, the Normal Continuance or Unity of

A s of September 30th, 2011, there were 104,236 children in public foster care waiting to be adopted. 1,946 children wait in the state of Missouri. The states of Texas and California have 13,481 and 12,881 children waiting respectively. Wyoming has only 127 foster children awaiting permanent homes.[xiii]

I was really beginning to feel settled, to feel at home. Just when I got used to the calm and good weather, that storm of disruption returned full force. Jack and Kaylee sat us down one day and told us that we were going to a new foster home. They hoped that this new family would adopt us.

I was stunned. I was furious. I felt that I had been completely betrayed. They were just giving up on us. They were just throwing us away. I could not believe that I had let my guard down. I started thinking to myself, "If I would have kept myself protected, I would have been able to take this news and deal with it a lot easier. I might have even seen it coming." I was so hurt that they had tricked me into finally opening up to them and accepting them as family, only to snatch away my comfort, my relief that I finally felt I belonged somewhere.

And so, they sent Jerry, Catina, and me to meet Lori and Randy Ross. I didn't want any part of it. I knew better. These people would just betray me too. This would be just another temporary home.

After a couple of years, they'd get tired of us and move us on, too. I wasn't going to be tricked into another false sense of security. I was ready this time. I knew what their agenda was, and I planned to not give them any satisfaction in destroying more of my life.

Jack and Kaylee had told us that we would have to stay with these strangers all weekend even though we had never met the Rosses before. I was so nervous when we arrived at the Ross house. I felt scared, trapped, and abandoned, all at once.

The Ross house was outside of Kansas City in a suburb called Blue Springs. But that semi-rural setting was the only thing similar to Jack and Kaylee's. There was what seemed like a million people there. You couldn't even keep them all straight. Within the first hour of us arriving, we were jumping on the trampoline, and Jimmy, one of the little boys, had bitten Jerry on the butt. Jerry started screaming. I was thinking, "This is too crazy for me. There are way too many kids in this family. I have to get out of here." It was ridiculous, and I did not want to stay with these people.

As the weekend progressed, I began to see some positives in the Ross household. There was a ton to do. There were kids to play with. There was always something going on. It might have been a good place to go for an overnight. It was sort of fun. But I certainly didn't want to live there.

When we came back to Belton, we had another family therapy session. I could tell at this point that Jack and Kaylee had really made up their mind about having us leave. I started acting out again. While we were in a family therapy session, I began to try and make trouble. Jerry did, too, because Jerry would do whatever I did since I was the older brother. We got sent to our rooms. I wasn't done. I wanted to act out more. I didn't want to just stay in my room, so I started running out of the room and up and down the small hallway making noise and trying to get Jerry to come out of his room and join me. But Jerry stayed put. Jack came down and told me that if I didn't stop, there would be consequences. At the point, I wanted to say, "You mean, like you might give me to another foster home?" But instead of saying that, I just kept running up and down the hall and up the stairs making loud obnoxious noises. I kept saying things like, "Oh, I'd like to see you try." Kathleen Baggett, who was Jerry's therapist, was this young slender woman with long red hair; she was the therapist who was there that day for family therapy.

Kathleen came downstairs to warn me that if I didn't get myself under control, she would have to restrain my body for me. She spoke in such a calm tone that I knew she had to be bluffing. I couldn't grasp how this petite lady could possibly think that she was going to get me under control. I remember saying something like, "Right. That's not happening," and sure enough, she got me into a restraint and held on tight. It was the first and only time I'd ever been restrained, and I was not giving up. I started flailing around, and cursing at both of them and telling them how dumb and obviously stupid they were, and how I hated them with everything in me. It was all the anger I could muster up, all the feelings I had buried down inside me. It felt like there was a hurricane of rage flowing through me. Exploding out of me.

My own personal inner storm raged: every released insult a thunderclap, every bit of misery a bolt of lightning, every torment an explosion trying to break free of Kathleen's grip. I would show them that I didn't need them anymore. This storm that I had tried so many times to keep under control was now making up for lost time and missed opportunities.

After about twenty to thirty minutes of me letting the storm have its way, it finally subsided. I calmed down and went to my room and collapsed into sleep, exhausted and spent from my outburst of pure rage. When I woke up, I found out that Jerry and Catina had gotten to go to the Belton carnival, and that I had been left at home as punishment for my loss of temper. How did that feel?

After that outburst, things got easier in the house. I tried to come to terms with the fact that I was leaving, and I tried to suppress any feelings of sadness or anger. I didn't think there was a point in expressing how I truly felt since the outcome was still going to be the same.

With some perspective, it's become clear to me that even though I lived with Jack and Kaylee for two years, I never felt that they were mother or father figures to me. I felt that they were more like guardians who cared for me greatly. I started to open up more with Jack and Kaylee, but I never completely let my guard down. I was still under the impression that everyone was out to take care of themselves and it was just a matter of time before I figured out what their motives were. Before I left Jack and Kay's, I started to get more of a familial bond with them, but it was closer to how I felt about my grandparents. It wasn't bad to feel that way, but there was always a void I felt with them, a feeling that I was missing a key bond that I could only ever get with a mother and a father figure in my life. I know that Jack and Kaylee cared for me. Of that, I have no doubt, at least not now, but it was like we had this unspoken understanding that my stay with them was temporary, and that the best thing they could do for me would be one of the hardest things for me to cope with.

After our first weekend with Lori and Randy Ross, we all went back to Belton, and Jerry told his therapist how much he hated it. He absolutely did not want to go. He let them know that he didn't want to move away, and they listened. Jack and Kaylee decided they wanted to keep Jerry. That sparked a whole new chain of issues for me. My mind was racing with thoughts: "How dare they give Catina and me up, but keep Jerry?" I kept thinking, "What's so special about him? How could they break Jerry and me up when we had been together since he was born?" We were only 18 months apart, so all of my memories had Jerry in them. I wasn't going to leave him! I was feeling so many different things, and so much anger and hatred towards them for doing this. But I had no choice. I wasn't given a vote. Catina and I had to move away and leave him behind. They wouldn't keep us. I had to let Jerry go.

INTEGRATION

An Act or Instance of Combining into
an Integral Whole

One of the most challenging parts of the idea of moving to the Ross house was knowing that there would be so many other people. The idea of sharing the attention with so many more people, not just Catina and Jerry but a bunch of other kids, was not appealing to me. With so many people there, the Ross house reminded me of an orphanage from a movie, or a smaller version of Crittenton, the treatment facility I had been to and hated. It seemed like a place for all the kids that no one else wanted. I didn't understand why they couldn't find us a different family.

It felt like no one there really wanted us, either. The older kids seemed obviously out to get me and Catina, and I got the distinct impression that they didn't want us in their family. I kept thinking, "This isn't going to work, I really want to leave this place." I kept calling my therapist, Helen, and asking her to please, please get us a new family. To please find us somewhere else, because I just didn't like it there. She kept telling me to try to stick it out.

Then we started having family therapy, which to me seemed like family gang-up-on-Catina-and-Ron time. We weren't doing anything wrong, and they were all complaining about everything we did or didn't do. I remember crying a lot during those therapy sessions but thinking I was hiding it from the rest of the family. My version of hiding it was putting a pillow over my head. I suspect, now, that they were very aware of my response.

I really believed they hated me. It felt like they were picking me apart, that everything I did or didn't do was wrong. Everything they said hurt, hurt my feelings, hurt my pride.

One time, one of my older brothers told me to stop looking at him, and I didn't. He came over and pushed me into the wall. I got up and ran to my room and started bawling. I couldn't stop. Finally, I snuck out and called Helen. I told her to get me out that house immediately. I told her what happened and explained that I just couldn't live in a place like that. She told me that I had to go and tell Lori what had happened and give her the chance to handle the situation. I was furious, but she wouldn't budge.

I waited until I was done crying. I went to Lori and said "Lori, uhm..." then I started crying again. She had a look of clear perplexity on her face, but she didn't say anything until I had finished crying. Then I was able to tell her that I had been pushed. Her face moved from confusion to annoyance as she yelled for the boy who had pushed me to come into the kitchen. When he came into the kitchen, Lori asked him if he had pushed me, and when he said that he had, she then told him to keep his hands to himself.

When another one of the kids overheard what was happening, he looked at me and said, "Is he really crying?" and he gave a look that said: "How pathetic."

I'm not even sure what I expected to happen. I think I wanted Helen to swoop in and take me somewhere else, a place where I could be the sole focus, where no one would ever do anything that might upset me. The push was troubling and disconcerting to me, but it didn't cause me any physical damage. It wasn't that big of a deal. But it was to me, or maybe I wanted it to be. When Lori reprimanded him, it kind of burst a balloon. She didn't pretend it was acceptable, she didn't hurt him back, but at the same time, I didn't get what I wanted. Still, on some level, I knew what he did wasn't really that serious, that my reaction was a bit extreme. Looking back on it now, if I had witnessed that event happening today at the house, I would be truly shocked to see someone crying over being pushed. I wouldn't be shocked to see someone telling on whoever pushed them. But such a strong response to an admittedly inappropriate but pretty everyday part of having brothers would leave me with a "how pathetic" look on my face as well.

I want to make this as clear as possible: it's not that the Ross family allows abuse. But being in the Ross family forces you to really look at what matters versus what's part of being in close quarters with lots of different people and personalities. We are an eclectic and varied group of people who have been through tough things and have survived, or are in the process of surviving those difficulties. We are very tough-skinned. Being part of this family means you are going to have to deal with sarcasm and chaos and people getting in your face, your space, and your mind. Things like being pushed don't happen that often among us older kids, but whenever I have witnessed confrontation in the house, it has never been life-threatening. I know what life-threatening looks like. I always know that the two people fighting in this household will be over it just as soon as it started, and they'll probably be jumping on the trampoline half an hour later.

When I first arrived, I was so sensitive to what the other kids said or did or how they looked at me. I was really convinced that they all hated me. Because of that, I let them hurt my feelings really easily. But as I stayed with the Ross family, my skin began to thicken up. It just comes with the territory of being a Ross. Everyone is so sarcastic that you have to stay on your toes. After a while, it became second-nature to just retort to a sarcastic remark. And as one of us with natural sarcastic tendencies, I soon learned to excel. There were limits to how you used words as well, but within those limits, I began to realize that I could hold my own. I never had to worry about being beaten up or getting yelled at for just being a kid.

Somewhere in this process, it became obvious to me that the family didn't hate me. What they wanted was for me to be sane enough, strong enough, secure enough, to be able to make my way in the world. It was time to learn how to come through my past experiences, not stay stuck in them, and how to move out into the real world as a full and active participant. No one is going to walk on eggshells around you at the Ross house, but the real world doesn't do that, either. They wanted me to succeed in the real world, not in just a safe environment of therapists and counselors and those who carefully tracked every word.

Over time, I grew aware of the family's love for me—for all of me, not just the well-behaved Ron, but the loud and obnoxious one, the one that wanted to control things, the one who might be a bit of a manipulator. I really began to know that I was going to stay with the Ross family, that eventually, they would adopt me, that I was a Ross. When I realized that I had finally found a permanent home, MY permanent home, I decided I wanted to get rid of every part of me that was related to my past life, including my name.

So I went from being Ronald Lee Bass, Jr. to being Nathan Daniel Ross. And I felt like a completely new person. I started a new school and a fresh life. I wanted to make the best of it. I wanted to have a new life of my own choosing. The Ross family didn't insist that I change my name. When the Rosses adopt those old enough to make the decision for themselves, they are encouraged to really think that through for themselves.

The decision to stay came, and I was in a middle school where most of the cliques were already formed. I didn't know where I belonged. I had a hard time motivating myself to complete schoolwork and to study for upcoming tests. Then Susie Nettleton came into my life. She was a nanny for the Ross house, and she decided to become my mentor as well. Susie took me under her wing and tried to help me get caught up in school. She set up a reward system to help me get all my assignments turned in for a week. She would allow me to go buy things or go to the movies as my reward. Of course, if I didn't turn in assignments, I would lose privileges. I remember feeling so great when I got to accomplish those things. I would have objected to the characterization at the time, but I see now how much I needed the discipline, the immediate rewards (or loss of rewards) and the focus-provided structure to start moving my life in a more positive direction.

I remember one time that I slipped (well, there were a few times). I had not turned in my assignments, but I really wanted to go to the movies to see *Matrix Reloaded*. Zach, Susie's husband, was going to take me to see it if I got all my work done that week. Well, I didn't want them to find out that I hadn't done my assignments, so I had Catina forge the signatures of the teachers, and I turned it in to Susie. She accepted the signatures and let me go to the movie. I thought that I had gotten away with it until a couple of weeks later when grade cards came out. I had a couple of Fs on my report card. My parents realized I had been lying about turning my work in. I knew they were going to have to tell Susie.

I couldn't look Susie in the face that day. I went down into my parents' room, and I stayed on the computer the whole time she was working there, because I didn't want to look at her. I knew how disappointed she would be with me for not doing my work and betraying her trust in me. Towards the end of her shift, she came downstairs and said to me, "We're going to have to talk about this, and there's going to have to be a consequence." And I just said, "Uh huh. I know." Then she left. The funny thing about it is there never was a punishment, and we never did actually talk about my report card, but the look of disappointment that she gave me was enough to back me get back on track, and I got my work taken care of.

Shortly after moving in with the Rosses, I got off my medication. They took me off the Risperdal and the Zoloft, and there was really no dramatic change in my behavior because I didn't really need to be on the medication at this point. But I remember after I got off the medication, seeing a picture of myself, and it was literally the first time that I had ever seen myself as a fat person. I don't know how I managed to not see it when I lived with Jack and Kaylee, but I was a big, big boy, and everyone teased me about it. I remember getting so depressed about how fat I was that I got up into the medicine cabinet and tried taking a handful of Zoloft pills because I wanted to die. I was so sad that I was so fat and that everyone was making fun of me on top of my feeling like I wasn't wanted.

The pills did nothing, and I remember going to Helen and saying, "Promise you're not going to tell anyone if I tell you this." I told her that I tried to kill myself with the medicine, and, of course, she explained that she was obligated to tell my mom. I was terrified of what Mom would do. I remember thinking, "Oh, God. She's going to kill me." But my mom just calmly said, "Don't do that. Don't do something that stupid. You don't want to end your life. Don't get into the medicine to do something like that. That's not smart." I was so relieved. It had only been a couple years since I had lived with Mary, and I was still apprehensive and thought that getting into trouble meant I was going to get beaten. Jack and Kaylee never spanked me or anything like that, but I was scared that Lori or Randy might. I was scared that I would get beaten with an extension cord or belt buckle, which was not the case, but it took me a while to adjust to the realization that beatings, like the ones I was used to, weren't a natural family thing.

After getting off the medication, it didn't take long before I dropped all the weight that I had gained. That extra weight had greatly affected my physical abilities. I had to quit the soccer team when I lived with Jack and Kaylee, because I wasn't able to keep up with the kids, or run around, and I felt like I was more of a hindrance to the team than anything else. Then I tried Karate when I moved in with the Rosses, and I had to quit it because I couldn't make it around the little square that they had us run around for warm-ups. I couldn't do it for five minutes without getting extremely tired and falling way at the back and having the kids laugh at me. I couldn't do the karate kicks or anything.

When I lost all the weight, however, I tried it again. Even though I didn't end up sticking with karate the second time around, it wasn't because I couldn't do it. It was just because I didn't want to. It was nice seeing myself look like other kids. I liked being skinny. I liked looking decent. When I went back to school my freshman year, a lot of people were wondering what happened—if I was anorexic or something, which I wasn't—but I got the flu and didn't eat for the time that I was sick, and I started to lose weight faster than normal.

When the kids would ask me what happened that made me lose so much weight, I just told them that I swam a lot over the summer. I didn't want to tell them that I used to be on medication; I didn't want it to get around school and then have everyone think that I was some kind of crazy person.

After we moved to the Rosses' and became a little more comfortable with them, I began to try to bend the rules, to test the limits. I got more comfortable with knowing that if I got in trouble, there'd be groundings and stuff, but I wouldn't get beaten or starved.

One day, in particular, I was pretending to be sick from school so that I could stay home for the day. Well, Natalie or Tyler, who are my handicapped brothers and sisters, one of them was sick and in the hospital, and my mom was at the hospital with the sick sibling. My aunt Karen, who is Lori's sister, was in charge of watching everyone who was home until my dad got off work. Aunt Karen knew that I was homesick for the day. About a half hour after she got there, I decided to go out to the living room and watch TV. She stopped me and turned off the TV. She told me that if I was sick, I really should be lying down in bed and resting. I explained to her that I was fine and that I didn't need to rest anymore, but she insisted that I go back to my room. That made me mad, so I wanted to call my therapist and talk to her about it. I refused to go. She grabbed me, turned me around, walked me back to my room and told me to stay in there.

I thought I was going to explode because I was so angry with her. And then my dad came home early and told me I could come out of my room and watch TV. I remember thinking, "Ha. I just shoved that in your face, Karen." I kept thinking how she must have hated knowing that she wasn't the boss of me, and that my dad let me watch TV after she told me I couldn't.

After I got adjusted to the house, I began to see that Karen was the one who was never afraid to put any of the children in their place. I have a lot of brothers and sisters in my family, and there are a few of them who are pretty spoiled. But when Aunt Karen's there, she doesn't play around. She gets things done, and you obey, or you pay the consequences. I love that about her.

Starting my freshman year, I did the things I needed to do. I worked hard and was able to complete school with decent grades. I had more friends, which gave me more confidence to try things. I joined the forensics team, which was like acting except with a lot of different rules and categories. I began going to forensics tournaments. Then I began winning tournaments, getting first place in dramatic interpretations, getting places in duo interpretations, qualifying in State, and winning my district. All of these things helped to improve my confidence, and I was really enjoying it. At the same time, I began doing theatre and acting in plays. Being involved in plays made me realize that acting was what I really wanted to do with my life. When it came time for graduation, I applied and was accepted to Northwest Missouri State University.

Catina didn't adjust well at the Ross house. I think there were a lot of unresolved issues between her and our biological mom, Mary, that she just never got closure on. While the Ross family adopted Catina, too, she never really accepted that this was her new family. Shortly after her high school graduation, Catina moved out.

Catina was mad because she was out late one night, and she knew that when she came home, she was going to be grounded. So, she decided that instead of dealing with her consequence, she would just run away. She moved in with her boyfriend's family. We didn't see her for a very long time afterwards, but we knew where she was and that she was safe.

For a long time, none of us heard from her, but then one day, she called to tell me that she was having a baby. Catina promised to keep in contact with me, so that I would know when she had the child. About nine months later, I got a call telling me that Catina had had her baby, and that she wanted me to come see her at the hospital. Susie and I went to the hospital that day, and we got to see Ajani, my new nephew. He was the cutest thing. I couldn't believe that I had a biological nephew in my life.

I began thinking about what had seemed special when I was living with Mary, or being so excited about going trick-or-treating with Jack and Kaylee, and now I was the uncle of a handsome baby boy. Joy filled my heart as I looked at where life had led. I was so happy that I had survived and was now seeing this new life in the world.

I got an email a little while ago from Jack and Kaylee saying that Catina had given birth to another baby. His name is Arion (pronounced r-e-yawn). A little over a year after receiving that email, Catina and I came back into contact with each other. I talk to her on a regular basis, and she and her new family are doing well.

Jerry still lives with Jack and Kaylee, though he's at school now. We are going through a phase right now where we just really don't get along at all. I think we both want different things in life, and we just seem to clash, and it seems like he tries to put everything that has to do with his past behind him. Now, he's almost like an only child, and I think he likes the thought of not having to have any memory of past traumas. I think that's another reason why we don't connect like we used to. It's disappointing. Since I first started writing this, Jerry has graduated high school and now lives in another state where he works in a factory. I hope to stay in contact with him, but I also realize the importance of him having his own space.

I find that I have a better relationship with my adopted siblings than I do with my biological ones. It's kind of depressing because Catina and Jerry are the only ones that can ever completely understand what I have been through. Still, I know that we are all in different places right now in life, and I just hope that in time we can reconnect and be a family again.

From the time I moved in with the Rosses up through my high school years, the only sibling that I have had a constant, instant connection with is my younger sister Emily. From the time that I arrived at the Rosses', Emily was nice and welcoming to Catina and me. She thought I was smart and funny. She seemed genuinely excited that I was there.

Now that I'm older, I have gotten closer to some of my brothers and sisters who are older than I am. They were in high school when I arrived, and they all had lives of their own. It felt like they didn't really have time for me, but Emma did. Even though she was Lori and Randy's biological child, she tried to see past that and just look at her siblings as if they had always belonged. Emily, or Emma as she is most often referred to, was really the first person who made me feel that I belonged with the family. I don't know if I would have adjusted to the family if Emma hadn't been part of it, and I don't know if anything could come between Emma and me.

Now that I am an adult, I can relate better to my older brothers and sisters. They even ask me to hang out with them, which is hard for me to get used to, because I'm so used to not hanging out with them except for family get-togethers. There was a definite divide in the Ross family between the older kids and the little kids, and a few of us landed in the middle. I suspect I'm now officially one of the older ones, and it's nice to have them want me around. But even to this day, there are times when I feel a bit out of place with the family. I suspect it's something that helps keep me grounded.

After I graduated high school, Jack and Kaylee offered to pay for my college tuition. If they hadn't done that, I wouldn't have been able to go to a university. It was really nice knowing my first two years were paid for. And they helped pay for my rent in the apartment I was staying in. When I joined a fraternity, they helped pay for that, too. They did so much that I didn't have to have any debt when I graduated college. It was really a wonderful gift and a truly grand gesture on their parts. They owed me nothing, and I didn't expect anything from them. I will always be thankful for their hospitality and love, and for this wonderful opportunity that I might not have had otherwise...that I WOULDN'T have had otherwise. It also showed me that they still cared, deeply. To be honest, there was a time when I wasn't really sure they did, especially because they didn't choose to keep me. But I'm beginning to realize that even that decision was made based on what was best for me, though it might not have felt like it at the time.

In our first therapy session at Midtown, after moving to the Rosses', I got to see Jerry for the first time. I was still angry that Jack and Kaylee kept him, so I tried to make him jealous. I told him that moving to the Ross house was the best thing ever because there were lots of kids and they had lots of money, and we got to do lots of cool things. I told him how they were going to get me a cell phone, even though they really weren't. I just wanted to make him jealous. And I don't think it even fazed him. I remember telling him those things with the hope that he would feel like he made a bad decision for not sticking with us and being part of the family like he was supposed to. Some ideas die hard.

REFLECTION

An Image; Representation; Counterpart; a Thought Occurring in Consideration or Meditation

Since ancient times and in all human cultures, children have been transferred from adults who would not or could not be parents to adults who wanted them for love, labor, and property. Adoption's close association with humanitarianism, upward mobility, and infertility, however, are uniquely modern phenomena. ...

In the United States, state legislatures began passing adoption laws in the nineteenth century. The Massachusetts Adoption of Children Act, enacted in 1851, is widely considered the first "modern" adoption law. Adoption reform in other western industrial nations lagged. England, for example, did not pass adoption legislation until 1926. ...

During the twentieth century, numbers of adoptions increased dramatically in the United States. In 1900, formalizing adoptive kinship in a court was still very rare. By 1970, the numerical peak of twentieth-century adoption, 175,000 adoptions were finalized annually. "Stranger" or "non-relative" adoptions have predominated over time, and most people equate adoption with families in which parents and children lack genetic ties. Today, however, a majority of children are adopted by natal relatives and step-parents, a development that corresponds to the rise of divorce, remarriage, and long-term cohabitation.

Conservative estimates (which do not include informal adoptions) suggest that five million Americans alive today are adoptees, 2-4 percent of all families have adopted, and 2.5 percent of all children under 18 are adopted. Accurate historical statistics about twentieth-century adoption are, unfortunately, almost impossible to locate. A national reporting system existed for only thirty years (from 1945 to 1975), and even during this period, data was supplied by states and territories on a purely voluntary basis.

We do know that adoptive kinship is not typical. Families touched by adoption are significantly more racially diverse, better educated, and more affluent than families in general. We know this because in 2000, "adopted son/daughter" was included as a census category for the first time in U.S. history.

Since World War II, adoption has clearly globalized. From Germany in the 1940s and Korea in the 1950s to China and Guatemala today, countries that export children for adoption have been devastated by poverty, war, and genocide. Because growing numbers of adoptions are transracial and/or international, many of today's adoptive families have literally made adoption more visible than it was in the past. But total numbers of adoptions have actually declined since 1970. In recent years, approximately 125,000 children have been adopted annually by strangers and relatives in the United States.

Modern adoption history has been marked by vigorous reforms dedicated to surrounding child placement with legal and scientific safeguards enforced by trained professionals working under the auspices of certified agencies. In 1917, for instance, Minnesota passed the first state law that required children and adults to be investigated and adoption records to be shielded from public view. By midcentury, virtually all states in the country had revised their laws to incorporate such minimum standards as pre-placement inquiry, post-placement probation, and confidentiality and sealed records. At their best, these standards promoted child welfare. Yet they also reflected eugenic anxieties about the quality of adoptable children and served to make adult tastes and preferences more influential in adoption than children's needs.

Since 1950, a number of major shifts have occurred. First, "adoptability" expanded beyond "normal" children to include older, disabled, non-white, and other children with special needs. Since 1970, earlier reforms guaranteeing confidentiality and sealed records have been forcefully criticized and movements to encourage search, reunion, and "open adoption" have mobilized sympathy and support. The adoption closet has been replaced by an astonishing variety of adoption communities and communications. Adoption is visible in popular culture, grassroots organizations, politics, daily media, and on the internet.

Adoption history illustrates that public and private issues are inseparable. Ideas about blood and belonging, nature and nurture, needs and rights are not the exclusive products of individual choices and personal freedoms. They have been decisively shaped by law and public policy and cultural change, which in turn have altered Americans' ordinary lives and the families in which they live and love. [xiv]

A little while after we had been at the Rosses', it was either right before we were adopted or just afterwards, a news team came out to the house to do sort of a "Where are they now?" on the "Bass children." I remember that as one of the first experiences I had to talk to any kind of press or the public about my life. I was worried that it would be really hard, that I would sound silly, but once I started talking, it just came out naturally.

The interviewer wanted to see what our family was like, to see how we were doing, if everything was going well for us or not. After the interview, I began having doubts about the intentions of those involved. I began to think that maybe the people covering the story just wanted to do it so that they wouldn't have to feel guilty about the kind of life we used to have. When the news people came out to see how everything was, I remember thinking that if it got back to DFS, it would help them to feel like maybe they hadn't messed up so badly, because we turned out pretty decently. I kept thinking about how they would be comforted by the fact that we hadn't been damaged to the point where we would never be functioning members of society. The thought that all the pain and hard work of finding my way back from those mistakes and awful horrors would be washed away really upset me.

I think that people honestly need to realize that we got lucky. This isn't the kind of happy ending that most people get. Something needs to be done to make sure that life doesn't have to get as bad as it did for my siblings and me before someone steps in to help. It is very saddening to me to know that some children never get saved. I really want to get the message out to people that yes, it is possible to have a great life after going through something very traumatic. And yes, it's possible to feel like a normal person again. But we need people, adults, to take the right steps towards getting at-risk foster and adopted children (of all ages) the help they need and deserve. We have to make sure that the children get placements with families who will show them unconditional love and support.

During my senior year, I had another interview for a newspaper; it was another sort of "How are they now?" type thing. A man named Eric Adler came to the house and wanted to do a piece on me to sort of show my resilience after all these years. This was the first time I actually talked about things that had happened with the knowledge that people would be reading what I said. When the first people came out to interview me a few years before, it was more like just a "How was foster care?" and things like that, and I didn't really feel comfortable yet talking about Mary Bass. This time, I felt that I could talk at least a little bit about what my life used to consist of. I remember Eric wanting to come to my school because I was in a play, and he wanted to get a glimpse of my interactions with my peers, in order to show people how I was adjusting. I told him that I wanted him to try to do it in a way that it didn't make me stand out from everyone else. I told him that I wanted whoever it was that was supposed to come to my school to make it look like he was just intrigued by the whole cast.

Before the reporter came out to do the interview at my school, I had to talk to my director to make sure it was okay, and she told me that it was fine. I remember thinking the reporter wasn't being as covert as I wanted. He was making it a lot more noticeable that he was there for me. And it became very uncomfortable because people would come up to me and ask, "Why is this guy staring at you?" "Why is this guy asking you questions?" and things like that. I think at one point he even asked some of my friends questions about me.

Because of how uncomfortable the process with the reporters made me feel, I didn't think I would ever do something like that again. I didn't want people to feel sad or bad for me. But after the newspaper came out, it was a really good feeling to have people come up to me and talk about how well I turned out, and how proud they were that I made it as far as I had. Friends and peers and even teachers came and said something positive to me. It was a really good feeling, which made me wonder if I could start talking about my past and hopefully get people to see that it doesn't have to be the end of the world just because you go through something traumatic. I think that's probably when I started thinking about writing a book, about telling my story for real, not just answering a few questions.

AUTONOMY

Independence or Freedom, as of the Will or One's Actions; the Autonomy of the Individual

I still believe that if Mary had gotten the help she needed (knowing she might not have accepted it), things might have been different. I often find myself wondering if I am just looking for someone else to blame for Mary's choices or insanity. I wonder if times were really as good as I remembered them when my mom was on her own with us. Is my natural allegiance to Mary so great that I can't even blame her for something that I saw firsthand? I mean, Tony didn't force her to burn Larry and Gary; in fact, he wasn't even there when it happened. So can I really blame him for that? Should I have more hatred for her than I do? I don't know if I will ever have a set viewpoint. I don't know if all the brainwashing and instinct will ever leave me and allow me to see something about Mary that I can't see now. As I think about it, I'm not sure that I want to. I want, very much, just to be able to forgive Mary and move on. I'm told that I have to accept my anger at her, but I admit that so far, I've not been able to think about that, much less let myself feel it.

When I was at Jack and Kaylee's, I began to realize, intellectually, the faults of my mother, and I began working at accepting those flaws. I guess that part of me is still convinced that she couldn't fully help herself since she was crazy. She must have been crazy to do those things.

During my high school years with the Rosses, I tried not to think of my old life very much. I wanted a fresh start, and I didn't want anyone to know about the past that I came from. I had gotten to the point where I didn't want anyone feeling sorry for me or, worse, using what they knew about my past to try to hurt me in some way. I wanted to show people that I was not going to let my past dictate my future. I had no time to think about Mary. Thinking about her could have made me regress back to my feelings of helplessness and anger, and I couldn't afford to have that happen in my life.

I was finally starting to feel normal, and I liked that feeling too much to succumb to bad feelings about my past. Now that I am in college, I have started to think about Mary more. There is a growing desire for me to see her, partly because I want some answers as to why she did what she did. I find that I have a desire to see how her psyche works. I want to see if there are any traits in her that I can see in myself. There is always this looming fear that if I'm not careful, I can end up like her. I am always scared to get too angry because I don't know what I will do. There are times when I feel my temper rising, and I can see myself doing just about anything to the "culprit." It is one of the scars from my past that I still have to deal with and probably will have to deal with for the rest of my life.

But I think that the reason that I most want to see Mary is that I still have a desire to be with her.

Even after ten years, there is a part of me that wants to make sure that she is okay. I still feel that I am responsible for taking care of her and making sure that no harm comes to this woman that has caused so much harm in her lifetime. I don't know what the future holds for me as far as a relationship to Mary is concerned. As much as I want to have some kind of contact with her, I don't know if I am ready to do so. I have now been without Mary for half my life, and I don't know if re-establishing any kind of relationship with her is in my best interest right now. It's nice that I can finally make that decision for myself, though. I remember being told that I wasn't allowed to see my mom because it would only make things worse for me. Although I believe it would have been bad, back then, it made me want to see her even more. I didn't like being told that I couldn't have any contact with the person that gave birth to me. Now, at least, the decision is mine and mine alone. So far, I've decided not to reopen that door.

COMPETENCE

Sufficiency; the Quality of Being Competent; Adequacy; in Possession of the Required Skills, Knowledge, Qualifications or Capacity

Over three years is the average length of time a child waits to be adopted in foster care. Roughly 555 of these children have had three or more placements. An earlier study found that 33% of children had changed elementary schools five or more time, losing relationships and falling behind educationally.[xv]

Embracing new parents isn't an easy thing. Between Randy and Lori, my dad, Randy, was easier to accept. Because I never really had a father figure in my life, it wasn't that hard to allow him to fill that void. I remember thinking how lucky all of the kids in the Ross house were that they got to have a dad. I was also scared, though, and on guard, because I wondered if he was an abusive father or husband. I was worried that he would beat me or my sister, and that made me apprehensive of him. But after meeting Randy, I knew that he was going to be a cool dad.

One of the first memories that I have of Randy is a day when he had come home from work, and Emma asked if they could rent a movie from Blockbuster. Randy said yes and told her that he would take her, and I got to go with them. I was so happy that I got to be included in a family-type outing. When we got there, I got to give my input on what movie we were going to get, and when Emma picked out some candy in the checkout line, Randy asked me if I wanted to get something, too.

Randy has always been the calm one of my two parents; it takes a lot to rattle him. He tries not to get involved in the disciplining if possible. It usually takes a lot for him to get really angry, and when he is angry, whoever caused it usually knows right away that they have messed up. I always liked that my dad was so relaxed and collected. It made finally having a father really nice, and it made me really thankful that I ended up with the Rosses. I don't know if I am as close to my dad as most kids are with their fathers. I think part of the reason is the fact that he didn't enter my life until I was 13, and by that time, I was so used to not having a dad that I didn't know how to have one.

That is one of the things that I still regret but don't know how to fix. Maybe we will figure it out moving forward.

I was never a big sports person by any means, partly because I wasn't really good at any sports, but mostly because I had gone so long in life not knowing how to play any of them that when I went into foster care, I was too embarrassed to ask someone to teach me. That's not to say that playing or knowing sports is the only thing that father and son relationships are based on, but Randy is a bit of a jock. A lot of the kids connect with him over sports. I couldn't use that as a point of entry, and I really didn't see how to build a relationship, or even where to start. But over time, we are forging our own connections. Randy has always come to see my plays, and he asks me how life is going when I'm home. We also talk a lot more now when I'm home than we used to. I know that he loves me and wants me to do well in life, and that in itself is a nice change for me as for father figures. I would say I have a good relationship with my father, though I would like for it to be closer as we grow, and will try to make that a priority.

Accepting Lori as my mother took a lot more time. For some reason, it didn't dawn on me that Lori would become my mother until a while after I lived with them. I guess I thought that I would go the rest of my life without a mother, and that I would learn to deal with it. It made it even harder accepting Lori as my mother because she's white. As bad as I feel for saying it, I was really worried that people would judge me for having a white mother, and I was embarrassed by it. It wasn't until I had to write my Confirmation (faith statement) for church that I really felt Lori was my mother. I remember sitting at a counter in our kitchen at home trying to figure out what I was going to say to the congregation of our church during Confirmation, and I started to think about how God had impacted my life, how I was grateful for how he had allowed me to go on living and had given me a chance to have a normal life, and that's about when it hit me how I was blessed to have another chance at having a mother.

I was able to see how a real mother is supposed to act and how she's supposed to treat her children. That's when I knew that I was proud to call Lori my mother and glad that I got to do so. Between my parents, I have had more struggles with my mom. Getting in trouble for not doing school work, or staying out too late, or having a bad attitude—those were all things that we butted heads on, but they were also things that helped us have a relationship with each other. I remember my mom telling me one time, while she was scolding me for not doing my school work, that no matter what I do, she will always love me and will be there for me. At the time, I thought she was just saying words to try to get me to do what she wanted me to, but she's never given up on me or made it seem like she wished she hadn't adopted me. That really helped me to feel safe and like I belonged to the family.

I remember when I first came to the Rosses', I was scared that I would get spanked if I messed up because I saw that she did give spankings. Granted, these spankings were nowhere near the type of spankings I used to receive, but I had gotten so used to not seeing anyone get spanked at the shelter or at Jack and Kaylee's, that it caught me off guard.

But I was told that I was too old to get spanked and that I would just get grounded instead. That knowledge took a lot of my fear away, and so did the casual way it was conveyed. I guess I was scared that she would lose control one day just like Mary did, and then another kid would end up like Larry and Gary. But the way she said it was like, "That wouldn't be effective for someone your age." It made it seem like punishment was just a repercussion of your choices, not a threat of death.

Because we were so scared, Lori made it a real point to be aware of the types of things she said and did around Catina and me. She tried not to yell at the kids that she "was going to knock them out" or "kill them," because she didn't want us to think that those were actual possibilities. (Though I must admit I've said them to my own little brothers and sisters over the years, I guess it no longer seems like a real possibility when I say it.)

As time went on, I began to see how the family worked. Everyone was sarcastic to one another, but deep down, no matter what they said to each other, they would protect their brothers and sisters when they needed to. They might mess with you, but no one else would. It was the first time that I got to see how a normal family worked. How it wasn't the sole job of the older siblings to take care of everyone but how everyone worked together to try and make the house run smoothly. Sometimes it was just your job to be a kid. The parents took care of the parent things, and while we needed to do our part, it wasn't our job to take care of them.

It's so weird looking back on my life now. Everything almost seems like a distant memory or dream that I once had. It's hard to think about the life of Ronald Lee Bass, Jr. and then look at the life of Nathan Daniel Ross and see that they are the same life. When I think about it, I guess that's a good and a bad thing. On one hand, I guess that it means I am no longer so traumatized by my past that I can only think about what happened to me. On the other hand, I don't want to lose sense of where I came from. It's hard to describe the feeling, but the best way I can think of is to explain it by quoting George Santayana, "Those who cannot remember the past are condemned to repeat it."

Now I know that it might sound a little extreme in regard to my past, but it is one of the fears that I have. Not only do I fear it for myself but for all people because if I can forget something that traumatic and that it happened to me, I have to assume that other people will soon think of the tragedy as a distant memory as well, thus allowing history to be repeated. Writing this book has really helped a lot in capturing what I was starting to forget. I actually realized that there were things that I didn't know I still remembered. After reading this, I want people to leave with an understanding of the kind of lives that some children have to go through, and I want them to do their part to bring an end to it.

As I was going off to college, Joe Beck, a therapist for our family, suggested that I do a public speaking event that was coming up in a few months. He told me that I would have to talk about my life story. It would be the first time I had ever done that in front of an audience, and I didn't think I was ready at that point in my life. So, when he first brought it up, I just said, "No, there's no way that I want to do that yet. There's no way I'm ready for that." But he let me think it over. My mom kind of talked to me about it, and told me everything I'd have to talk about and asked me what I was worried about, what scared me about the idea.

Then I believe God opened up my heart. He allowed me to think about the possibility of helping others with my story. Suddenly, it made me want to do it. I was still scared and nervous, but I wanted to give it a try, at least to see how it would work out.

I remember going to that first public speaking engagement and sitting at the podium, nervous. I really didn't know if anyone was going to care about what I had to say. I was still just a kid (a late-teenage kid, but a kid). Why would anyone listen to me? But I gave my speech about my life anyway. At the end of the talk, the audience stood up and started clapping for me. Their responses were wonderful. They had heard me, what I had said mattered, and they were thinking about it. It was just the best feeling in the world. I felt like maybe I had actually helped change at least someone's life from just giving that speech. It was then that I realized that if I could do that every day, my life would be so happy and fulfilled. If I could make a difference, improve the odds, then everything might be worth it. And all I had was my story. But if I was willing to share what really happened to me and everything I want to do with my life, then maybe it would make a difference. Maybe it could get families help sooner. Maybe it could get more children into permanent families. Maybe it could motivate foster parents to keep their licenses. Maybe it could matter.

And maybe, just a little, I would feel like I was giving back to my brothers who gave up everything in order for me to live.

When people are moved or educated or even enraged by this story, by this life I have lived, I feel like I'm doing something to make everything that has happened to me worthwhile. I mean, yes, there were some truly bad things, but it made me who I am, and it helped me grow into the person that I am today. I now have an understanding about what the storms can be like – how far, and how bad those storms can get. If I don't do my part to bring back the sun in someone's life, who will?

IDENTITY

The Condition of Being One's Self or Itself, and Not Another; the Condition or Character as to Who a Person or Thing Is.

Moving on to college wasn't as hard as I had thought it would be. When the time finally approached for me to venture off on my own, I was excited. It reminded me of that day fifteen years ago when I got on the school bus, Batman lunch box in hand, setting off on a great adventure. I couldn't wait to experience what it would feel like to take care of myself. The first day moving onto the campus of Northwest Missouri State was the most nerve-racking. The drive-up to Maryville freaked me out. It was only an hour and a half away from Blue Springs, but it felt like it took forever to get there. I was so worried that I wouldn't remember the way home and therefore would be stuck in Maryville forever. When we got to Maryville, and I saw all of the people moving in, I became even more nervous as I began thinking about how easy it would be for me to get lost in the crowd.

I had known that a few people from Blue Springs were going to Northwest, but I wasn't sure when I would see them, so I was worried about what I would do up there by myself with no one to hang out with. After we finally got all of my stuff moved into my room, my parents took me to Walmart to get some things, and then we went to Burger King for a late lunch. While we were at Burger King, I texted one of my friends that I knew went to Northwest to see if she was back in Maryville already, and she told me that she wasn't going to Northwest anymore. That's when I got even more nervous. I was really worried that I was going to be alone, and school wasn't starting for a few more days. Finally, it came time for my parents to leave, and for the first time, it hit me that I was going to be on my own.

I began thinking about how I didn't want them to leave me. I hadn't even realized how attached I was to my family until I thought I was going to be alone. So there I was on my own when one of the RAs for my building came to my room and told me that a really good way to make friends is to leave my door open so that people knew I was in my room. He was right. After I went and got my laptop and came back to my room, a couple of guys came by and asked me if I wanted to go to dinner with them and then to the football game later on that night. I was relieved that I had something to do and I felt like I must not have been a complete loser.

After that first night, things got a lot easier for me. On the second day at Northwest, I had to go to a freshman seminar class. The classes were divided up by the majors that were chosen upon acceptance to Northwest, so I had to go to the one for my Theatre major. Of course, it was the day that I was running late, and I couldn't find what building I was supposed to be in. So when I finally got to the class, everyone was seated already, and they all looked at me when I entered. I felt so embarrassed for showing up late. It was not the kind of first impression that I wanted to give to these people that I was going to have to be around every day for the next four years. During the class, it was explained to us that we would have to go to various places over the course of the weekend to help us get to know the campus better. I also learned that I would be in the freshman seminar class for half of the first semester. Then we were taken over to the Theatre where we would normally have our freshman seminar class. Once in the class, we played some get-to-know-you games, and it really helped all of us open up to each other. From that point on, I spent almost all of my time surrounded by theatre people. Whether it was because of the plays that I was a part of or the parties that I went to, the Theatre became my home, and the actors and technicians became my Maryville family.

After school started, I decided that I wanted to join a fraternity. I had heard that joining a frat was the best way to make connections and friends. Since that was something that I was worried about, I figured that it would be a good choice for me. I got a lot of grief from the Theatre people because they said it was too difficult to do both theatre and be in fraternity, but I was determined to make it work out. I was in a play during rush week for the fraternities, so I had to narrow it down to only a couple of houses that I would be interested in. I ended up only being able to go to the TKE house during rush week, so they were the only ones that I got a bid from. It was a fun and challenging experience that, combined with Theatre, took up all of my time. I never felt like I was truly part of TKE, however, because I was so busy with the Theatre that I didn't have a lot of time to get to know my rush brothers. I also missed out on the really cool fraternity stories. I was determined to stick it out though, and I continued to rush and eventually was accepted into TKE as a Brother. Unfortunately, I didn't really have a lot of use for TKE by that point. Since I had spent so much time working on theatre stuff, the only people I hung out with were theatre people, so while I knew who my brothers were, I wasn't great friends with most of them. I eventually dropped TKE altogether, but it was still an experience that I'm glad I got to have.

I spent my freshman year of college majoring in Theatre. I tried out for plays and got to be in the Freshmen/Transfer show. Acting was something I loved, but at the same time, something didn't feel quite right. The college I was attending had a good theatre department, but I felt like I should be focused on film, not stage. That felt like what I ultimately wanted to do. I love acting, period. And stage is great, but film-acting is what I have a desire for. I've always been passionate about film. I started wondering what I was doing, and whether I was just going down a path because it was easier. I decided to try to get a degree in something I could use until I made it as a film actor. So, my sophomore year, I changed my major to psychology, and after a little while, I surprised myself by loving it. I really love analyzing people. I love analyzing myself. I'm pretty good at reading people, and I can figure some people out pretty easily, so I figured psychology would be a pretty good avenue for me. I have found that I'm also good at listening to people and helping them with their problems. There are lots of people who come up to me and ask for advice, so I figured if it's something I'm good at without a degree, then if I got some training, I could be even better. As time went on, however, I realized that I just didn't have the same passion for psychology that I have for acting. I sort of bounced back and forth trying to figure out what was right for me.

Over the next couple of years in college, I had lots of changes. I became a better actor, allowing me to get better roles in plays, which was a big turnaround from high school. The better roles helped me feel more confident that acting was the career that I wanted to pursue. I also began speaking publicly about my past and trying to help change the future of other children who experienced traumatic family lives.

I also got into my first serious relationship, with Alexandria.

Alexandria was the first person to talk to me during our freshman seminar class. We had become Facebook friends because, in high school, I was briefly dating one of her friends. When I first met Alexandria, she was in a relationship of five years with her boyfriend, so I didn't see us as ever having an intimate type of relationship. During my freshman year, Alexandria wasn't around a whole bunch because she spent most of her time with her boyfriend, but we had a couple of Theatre classes together, and we were both in the Freshman/Transfer play "John Brown's Body." It didn't really seem that we had a whole lot in common. I was a person who liked to go out and party. I had a sharp, caustic sense of humor, cursed a bit, and was kind of wild. I was really enjoying being away from home. On the other hand, Alexandria was raised in a white, extremely conservative Christian environment and thought that partying was a waste of time and sinful. It wasn't that I thought she was necessarily wrong, but it just put us at opposite ends of the spectrum. The summer after our freshman year, however, Alexandria broke up with her boyfriend and came back for her sophomore year a new person. She was a lot more open to everyone, personable and seemed happier. She still held on to her beliefs, but it seemed that a wall was taken down.

I first started talking to Alexandria not because I was looking for a relationship with her but to help one of my other friends who had a crush on her. I tried to suggest ways that he could approach her, and I tried to figure out how interested she was in him. Alexandria told me that for various reasons, she wasn't sure that he was for her, and I honestly tried to change her mind. What I didn't expect was to develop a crush of my own. I became aware that I was able to talk to her openly because I wasn't looking for a relationship with her. I was honest and showed her the real me. After a while, I realized that I liked her, and I felt guilty and ashamed of myself. I told her how I felt and that I didn't want to ruin my friend's chances with her by trying to fight for her affection. Alexandria and I left the conversation at that and tried to go on being just friends. But the more we hung out together, the more we began feeling for each other. After some time, we decided that we did want to be together, and so she became my girlfriend. I thought that things were going to get simple after that, but I was in for a whole new mess of problems.

First, Alexandria's ex-boyfriend decided that he wanted her back, and so he tried pursuing her. When she made it clear to him that they were not getting back together, and she told him that she was with me, he tried to convince her that I was bad for her and that I was using her. Dealing with him and his accusations alone got us off to a rocky start. Then came Alexandria's parents. When I first met them, it was during the time when we were just friends. I remember they were friendly to me and seemed to like me. But after they realized that I was going to be dating their daughter, things changed. Her parents and her sister made it very clear that they didn't want us to be together. Alexandria is a beautiful, white woman. They didn't approve of our dating. Their warped perceptions about me made it really hard for me to connect with Alexandria, who deeply respects and loves her family.

Up until I started dating Alexandria, I forgot that people had problems with interracial couples. I had gotten so used to being in my family, where we look like a daycare center at the United Nations, that I had forgotten what the world could be like. Dealing with Alexandria's parents was hard and almost ended our relationship several times.

In the beginning of our relationship, there always seemed to be problems between us. She was afraid of getting hurt again, and I was afraid of opening up too much for fear that she would use what she knew against me. That was a constant struggle for us. Alexandria always wanted to know what was on my mind, and I hardly ever wanted to tell her. I was also very apprehensive about relationships in general because I had never had a girlfriend for a long period of time. Whenever it got to the point where I would have to open up, I simply checked out of the relationship and moved on. After a few months, I became nervous that it was only a matter of time before she would hurt me, so I pulled away, not wanting to give her a chance.

We still continued to see each other and had lots of good times together. We went on dates and just enjoyed each other's company, but something seemed to be lacking. Then came second semester of my sophomore year when we were both casts in the play "Metamorphoses." During rehearsals, things seemed to go from bad to worse. Even though we saw each other every day and she would stay with me at night, we were more distant than ever. The distance between us turned into paranoia and jealousy. We both began feeling like the other one was pulling away and wanting to be with other people. As this feeling increased in me, I became more and more detached from Alexandria because I felt she was going to leave me soon. There were times when I wanted to break up with her, but I didn't want to give her parents the satisfaction of thinking that they were right. So I did what I knew how to do best. I manipulated her emotions to try to make her break up with me.

As I expected, it worked. Alexandria told me that she thought we shouldn't date anymore. When she first said this, I thought to myself, "Thank God, it's over." I figured that I had to act like I was surprised though, so I asked her why she wanted to end our relationship. She told me that she felt that we weren't working because we didn't have a connection anymore. She thought that we were too distant from each other.

But what she said next changed everything in me. She proceeded to tell me that she had feelings for someone else. It was then that I knew that I was right all along about her and about people in general. My sense that it was a matter of time before she left me for someone else now seemed confirmed, and I felt stupid that I had allowed myself to get as close as I did to her. I had half a mind to curse her out and be done with the whole relationship, but something had changed. I found myself wanting her to stay, and I wanted to fix things and try to let her back into my life. At first, I thought it was mere jealousy. I simply wanted her so that no one else could have her, which I was prepared to get over. But the more I thought about our relationship, the more I realized that it was something deeper. However, the damage was done already. She had made up her mind that she wanted to be with someone else and even though we spent the next three days dragging out whether we should break up or not, in the end, it wasn't me that she chose. It hurt.

It was the first time that I had ever felt this type of emotion about someone that wasn't family. I had this immense feeling of abandonment. I didn't know how to handle what I felt. I became so angry with her for hurting me the way that she did that I wanted her to suffer more than I had ever wanted anyone to suffer before. The anger consumed me. I wasn't able to eat or sleep for about a week. I just kept thinking about everything that she had ever said to me, and I kept thinking about how it was all bullshit and that she must have only been using me as a rebound from her last boyfriend. I was also very angry with myself. I knew all along what would happen. I just knew, yet I allowed myself to bypass my instincts, and now I had to feel this unbearable pain.

Of course, I didn't want everyone else to see just how badly I was hurting, so I tried to pretend that everything was okay. I spent all of my time either in my room or hanging out with friends so that I didn't have to think about Alexandria as much. It didn't take me long to start moving on with life, though. One thing that I had gotten good at was suppression. After that first week of anger and sadness, I told myself that it was time to stop being so angry with her. I didn't like how it was making me feel, and I didn't like allowing another person to control my feelings that way. So, I wrote her a letter telling her that I was done being angry and that I was moving on.

Big talk. The second week apart was hardest because I thought about her all the time. It seemed like everywhere I turned, she was there. I didn't want her to think that I was miserable without her, so I laughed and joked around with friends and tried to have fun. Toward the end of the week, both Alexandria and I were invited to a campout along with other friends from the Theatre department. I texted Alex to ask her if she could bring my sleeping bag by my apartment so that I could stay the night at the campout. When Alexandria got there, I remember my stomach dropping. I was so nervous I didn't know what I was supposed to say or how I was supposed to act.

I told her that I was going to try to be civil about us not being together, and at that point, while she was standing in my bedroom door, I realized that I could do just that. I didn't feel immense hatred for her. I was sad still that we weren't together, but I didn't place the blame solely on her. She dropped off my bag and asked me how I was doing. I said that I was okay and proceeded to ask her the same. She said that she had been better, and I could tell that there was something that she wanted to say to me.

I asked her what she wanted to tell me, and she was hesitant at first, but I didn't want to give up. I was hoping deeply that she was going to tell me that her life was miserable without me and that she wanted to give us a second try. Still, I was afraid that wasn't it at all. Eventually, she did tell me that she couldn't stop thinking about me and how I seemed to be everywhere she went. We spent the next five hours talking about things we noticed about each other over the last two weeks and then came the hard topic... what do we do next? Even though I was glad to know that Alexandria wanted to give us a second try, I was also worried about whether it was the right thing to do. The seven months we were together prior to the breakup were so rocky that I wasn't sure that I wanted to go through that again. I was also fearful that she might find someone else mid-relationship like the last time and leave me again. After our long conversation, we decided to take things very slow and see where we would end up.

~

Although I have come a long way since 10-year-old Ronald, I still struggle with issues of my past. I can let people into my life to a certain extent, but it is difficult, and I am always ready to withdraw if I feel emotionally threatened. I still try to figure out what people's motives are and what they expect to get from me. It's one of the survival techniques that I still hold on to today. Even with friends, I find it hard to be completely myself for fear that they might take what they know about me and use it to hurt or manipulate me in some way.

Having that fear is one of the reasons that I considered not writing this book at all. I wasn't sure that I was ready for people to know the real life of Nathan Ross. Although I am not anywhere near as sensitive as I used to be, I still have some of the old fears. I find that the more I talk about my past and the more I speak publicly about the effects of child abuse, the more I feel okay with my life and feel that I am doing the right thing in letting people know where I came from and why I'm determined to do better for myself in regard to my future.

I don't know if I will ever be able to completely let my guard down for most people, but I pray that I am at least able to for a few. It might be one of the forever scars that I have with me. But I kind of think that it's a good thing, I think that having this "scar" will help me remember where I come from and what barriers I still have to overcome. I often fear that I will somehow forget why I do some of the things I do in life, like advocating for a better child welfare system, and that is something that I never want to forget.

I am thankful that I am in a place today that allows me to think about where my life had started, and that I can use it to motivate me to fight for a better tomorrow for myself and for others who don't have a voice or aren't able to help themselves. I think that as long as I don't let having my guard up control my life, it can be a valuable tool. I do believe that there is more work that I can do in letting it down, but I also believe time is often the best medicine for emotional wounds. I am proud to say that I have let my shield down enough to love and to be loved. I have been hurt from having my shield down, but I have also been rescued because of it. I won't let my past dictate my life negatively. I have come too far to regress to my former ways.

One of the driving forces behind my adult life and what I want to accomplish with it is a deep desire to have a family of my own someday. When I first thought about it after going into foster care, I told myself that I never wanted to have a family because I was terrified that I was going to end up like my mother, Mary. But as the years have gone by, I feel more and more confident that being a father is not only something that I could do but something that I could do well. I'm not saying that I want to have kids right now or anytime soon really, but I know that I do want to have a family and I want to be there for my family. I know that I don't ever want my kids to grow up not knowing their father, and I know that I would do everything in my power to protect them. I'm aware that part of my desire for a family comes from having to take care of my siblings, and even Mary to a certain extent, at such a young age. The haunting fear that I might turn out like Mary still comes up at times, but I have people in my life who believe in me and encourage me daily, and that helps me get over my fears at least for the most part. I also have a network of brothers and sisters to hold me accountable, which, if you have met my family, you know is a huge asset.

Being able to finally have the kind of family that I have right now, with both a mom and dad, and all of my brothers and sisters, has really shown me that it is possible for people in bad situations to come out of them and turn their lives around. But they can't do it alone. I look forward to giving the kind of love that I have received over these past thirteen years to a family of my own someday. I believe family is an essential part of life and I feel sorry for those who never get to know how it feels to have people who care about them. That is another reason I wanted to write this book. I hope it gives people the courage needed to help take in children without permanent homes and to love those children and give them everything they were missing with their previous family.

People often assume that it's too hard adopting older kids out of foster care because they are too damaged, and they probably can't be fixed. Well, I'm here to tell all who believe this that they are wrong. Yes, it is hard, very hard to raise foster children, especially ones who are older, but they are still children, and they still need to feel loved. Even though they might have severe issues—in fact, they almost certainly do—if they have someone they know is going to stick around and help them through the hard stretch, that just might be all they need to turn their lives around. Everyone has the desire to be loved by somebody, no matter how old they are or what kind of situation they have come from.

I hope there comes a day when I don't have to feel that I was one of the few lucky ones because I found my forever family even though I was older. I hope that one day, every child that goes into foster care will get to find their forever family – a place to start over and be loved.

INDIVIDUALISM

The Principle or Habit of or Belief in Independent Thought or Action

Late Fall 2012

It has been five years since I started the journey of putting all of my memories and thoughts on paper, and a lot has changed in that time. When I first started the process of writing this book, Alexandria and I were still dating, and I wasn't quite sure where that relationship would lead. Eventually, we got married, but unfortunately, it didn't last long. Many of the problems we faced in college followed us into our marriage, which ultimately got to a place where we couldn't go any further together. Still, there were pieces from that relationship that have shaped the man I have become, and so I had to challenge myself to cherish the good times and learn from the bad.

In July of 2011, I started working at my mom's nonprofit agency, Midwest Foster Care and Adoption Association, as a youth programs manager. The more involved I became in the child welfare system, especially through my public speaking, the more I realized that helping create systemic change is where my passion lies. It has been an amazing experience so far and one that has really challenged me to think of ways to help children currently going through the foster care system.

One of the first programs I ever developed was a mentoring program that serves older youth in the foster care system, provides them with opportunities to have successful transitions into adulthood. Each year, approximately 25,000 young adults, for whom no permanent placement has been found, exit the foster care system by "aging out"—simply by reaching a certain age. The challenges faced by young adults aging out of foster care are abundant. Many of these challenges relate to the lack of a support system that generally arises from long and stable membership in a family and community.

Other challenges relate to dealing with the trauma associated with childhoods marked by neglect, abuse, or family separation. Ultimately, young people aging out of foster care often lack a financial, social, and emotional safety net that allows them to make and learn from mistakes. With these challenges, not surprisingly, poor outcomes for this transitioning population of young adults are prevalent and well-documented. Various studies show that only 3% of youth aging out of foster care will graduate from college, up to 35% will experience homelessness soon after aging out, up to 40% will become parents by the age of 20, up to 25% will be incarcerated, and many will struggle to find jobs that pay a livable wage (The Pew Charitable Trusts, May 2007).

I believe that a supportive and caring adult role model is crucial for youth transitioning out of the foster care system. With this support, foster kids are given the chance to build stable, trusting relationships while acquiring vital independent living skills. As such, the use of mentoring programs for older adolescent foster youth represents a particularly beneficial prevention strategy that may help prevent negative outcomes as youths emancipate from the foster care system and make the transition into young adulthood. When you've been through so much, sometimes it's hard to believe anyone understands or accepts you. There is a lot of power in looking one of these young adults in the eyes and saying, "This happened to me, too." It can unlock doors and open minds.

I decided to start with mentoring because I knew how beneficial it was for me to have someone in my life that I didn't feel had an agenda. That is one of the main complaints that children in the foster care system have. They don't yet see the benefits of the professionals in their lives. While critical and well-intentioned, professionals are often viewed as people just trying to get something out of them. Foster kids are quickly aware that these adults will leave once they have received what they are looking for or situations and assignments change.

I wanted to be able to provide an opportunity for older children, at risk of aging out, to have someone they can connect with and talk to in times of need, especially when they get out into the adult world. I wanted each of these kids to have someone in their lives who has the flexibility to try and be there beyond a case assignment or a crisis diagnosis. The first year of program operation went very well. We had a goal set of getting 25 mentors recruited and were fortunate to have surpassed that number, with 40-plus mentors having responded to the need in their community. Eventually, we were able to approach Big Brother and Big Sisters with our program model, and were fortunate enough to have them take the project on and grow it in ways that we could not. It is one of my dreams that mentors will be provided to each and every child that enters the foster care system. My hope is that each child will have at least one consistent person who will walk with them through the foster care process, providing guidance and support.

Between navigating a short marriage and figuring out my career path, I have had a lot to keep me busy. It is comforting to know that I don't ever have to tackle any of these challenges on my own. I've let go of a lot of the fierce self-reliance that marked my early years in the system. With an abundance of family and friends, I am constantly surrounded by people to motivate me and lift me up as I continue my journey to use the experiences of my life to pave a better future for other children affected by abuse and/or neglect.

~

When I first set out to write this book, my aunt, Karen advised me to get ahold of my records from being in foster care to help fill some of my memory gaps. A process that I thought would be fairly simple to achieve turned out to be quite difficult and really annoying. I spent a ridiculous amount of time trying to get access to my own files from the time I entered the foster care system until I was adopted. I'm sure some of that difficulty had to do with the systemic desire to protect itself from what was a deep and tragic embarrassment, which included me signing a waiver that stated that I would not disclose the details of what was in those files. Still, I was able to learn a lot as I reviewed the documents.

When I first started reading over the files covering my time in the foster care system, I mostly expected to find fuller detail on all of the information I already knew. I had spent the last three years recounting my story over and over again, and I was pretty used to the overall timeline of how events went down and the story behind each one. However, as I began reading over my case file, it seemed like I had accidently gotten someone else's story. Some of the events that I recalled were in there, but they were out of order from how I had always remembered and spoken about them.

For example, I always remember the only time that I was restrained as happening after we were told that we were moving to a new home two and a half years after being with Jack and Kaylee. The way I remembered it, I was so angry at the sudden betrayal that I refused to continue "family therapy" because they were no longer going to be my family. As I ran through the house trying to disrupt the structure that had been put in place, Kathleen, who was Jerry's therapist, told me that if I didn't get under control, they would do it for me. The reality is that this story actually happened within the first few months of living with Jack and Kaylee and was not a result of my feelings of betrayal towards them.

As I read through the pages that were turning my perceptions upside-down, a small feeling of anger came over me. I started to feel like someone must have messed with my file and rearranged things. It was easier to try to blame it on someone else than come to the conclusion that I had misremembered what was once such an important story in my life. I had always used the story of my restraint to show those I was speaking with the effects of children moving from home to home. I wanted to instill in my listeners the importance of permanency and how even well-behaved children would act out if they were disrupted. Instead, I was facing the harsh truth that I had a lot more baggage from being taken from Mary than I had realized.

As I continued reading the details of my first year in foster care, my anger turned into amazement. I couldn't believe all of the things that I was reading that I just didn't remember. It was like someone had used the story of my life as a template and added bits and pieces in that they thought would spice it up. I was slowly coming to the conclusion that I was that stereotypical kid in foster care that had extreme behavioral challenges and had to have constant attention. That wasn't how I remembered it. That wasn't how I experienced it at the time. I thought I was pretty normal even through the turmoil.

So, what does this mean? Why would my mind block out things that were not traumatic or hard to handle? I was suddenly filled with new questions, which included how I was going to tell my story from that point on. After taking some time to let all of the new information set in, and after talking with my aunt about my new discoveries, I was able to understand what I had really known all along, and that is that a child's memories are just that, the memories of a child. When I was ten, I was shaping my reality based on the traumas of my past and the expectations for my future. It was sort of like a filter, if you will. Everything that I thought about and stored for the long term had to deal with my acceptance of the past and my recovery. I think one of the main reasons that I don't remember the behaviors is because for me, at that point in my life, they weren't behaviors. They were the tools and processes that I used to make sense of the situation that I was in and to keep myself protected from further trauma. I believe that my mind only focused on remembering the situations that were overcome, while throwing out some of the means that I used to overcome those situations. Of course, this is all speculation, and I'm sure there is some therapist or other professional who will read this and come up with a different conclusion, but at this point in my life, that is the best one I can come up with.

So I guess the part that I would want the reader to take from this is that when dealing with foster children, it is really important that one be informed of the traumas that the child has suffered because those traumas affect how they perceive reality and how they go about making sure they survive. Take, for example, that fact that Mary used to starve us on a consistent basis. Now, when we came into foster care, we continued hoarding food just as we had done prior to coming into care. Someone who was unaware of the fact that hoarding used to be one of the ways we survived might look at us and think we were greedy children or children who wanted to take control of every situation and used food hoarding as one of those ways to gain control. As a result of this type of thinking, they might restrict when we could eat and give us punishments when they found us with food that we weren't supposed to have. That would obviously have made the situation worse. It would have resulted in us doing whatever we felt necessary to make sure that we could survive, in case they restricted our food to the point that Mary did.

On the other hand, a person who was trauma-informed, as Jack and Kaylee seemed to be, would have realized that we were hoarding not because we were trying to take control in the negative sense, but because we thought we still needed to hoard in order to survive. Someone with this type of trauma-informed perspective would be sure to reassure us constantly that we would always have meals in their house and that we didn't need to hoard food because starvation would never be used as a punishment. This constant reassurance would lead to feelings of safety and a realization that hoarding isn't needed for survival.

Looking at these files from the perspective of someone who works with foster and adoptive kids, I also realize that while in the depths of survival mode, a child's perspective or sense of connection with a well-intentioned adult may not make it through their filter. There were any numbers of people who interacted with me on an ongoing basis who I have no memory of, while others I will never forget. When this became clear to me, I wanted to apologize to everyone I didn't remember or whom I remembered differently. I don't know why my memory wasn't quantitative and accurate, but it wasn't, and I'm sorry if that has hurt anyone who tried to help me but didn't make it through the filter. But please don't stop trying!

I can't identify why certain people made an impact and others didn't, but I think that's the magic of it. Sometimes we connect, sometimes we don't. But if we don't keep trying, we know we won't. For me, as an adult working with these kids, I want to make sure I understand that the challenges in these children's lives often mean they can't see, feel, or accept the fact that others care about them. My job is to make sure I keep saying, demonstrating, and staying, so that when they can accept it, it's there for them.

~

One of the funniest things that people say to me after hearing my story is how proud they are that I am so normal and how they would never be able to tell that I was once in foster care. This is a statement that former foster children who have successfully transitioned into adulthood hear quite often. The truth of the matter is that although I do have a fairly "normal" life, I still have some lasting effects from the trauma that I suffered as a child, many of which I have just discovered.

When Alexandria and I were first engaged, many people told us that we should have pre-marriage counseling so that we could better understand what exactly we were getting into. We both agreed that it would be helpful and decided on a counselor who attended the church Alexandria's parents went to. During one particular meeting, our counselor told us that he wanted us to practice resolving conflict. He told us that people have a hard time processing conflict appropriately when their heart rate goes over 100 beats per minute, so he wanted us to have a discussion about a conflict we had in the past while hooked to a monitor so that we could see how our heart rate progressed and would, therefore, know when we needed to break from a conversation and come back to it at a later time. So, he hooked Alexandria to the monitor, and her heart rate was somewhere in the normal range for a resting heart rate. But when he hooked me up to the monitor, we discovered that the anxiety of the monitor alone raised my heart rate to just over 100 beats per minute. I was quite shocked and asked him why he thought that was. Now, we had talked about my past in previous sessions, so he was aware of my life situation. He told me that I still suffered from the anxiety of my past and that as a result, my body is constantly in fight-or-flight mode. I knew that I had anxiety to some extent, but I wasn't aware of how bad it was. He told us that conflict resolution was going to be more difficult for me because my body already started in a position where it can't process conflict well. He also told me that stressful events would likely make my heart rate increase even more and affect my day-to-day functioning.

I realized how right he was after I began having trouble sleeping. I found that I would wake up in the middle of the night with my brain in full-working mode. I had so many things going through my head that I wouldn't be able to fall back to sleep for hours. I really didn't want to put myself on medication for fear that my body would become dependent, but I needed some sort of aid to help me sleep. I began trying to find ways to focus my brain on other sources besides the events that were making me anxious, and I made an interesting discovery. I noticed that if I put the movie Fantasia on, I could go back to sleep relatively quickly. As weird as it may sound, the movement on the screen gave me something to concentrate on and the music playing allowed me to calm my brain down enough that I could fall back to sleep. For about a month, I would have trouble sleeping and would turn to that movie for peace. I still have times when my anxiety will wake me up in the middle of the night. Even though it has been 16 years since I lived with Mary, my body still hasn't fully recovered, and I'm not sure it ever will.

My high anxiety isn't the only problem that I have recently discovered. I began to realize that I still have sort of a hoarding problem when it comes to food. When I lived with my parents, I was never aware of it because there were so many children that food never lasted long. I then lived on my own and just assumed that I wasn't as hungry as I thought when I bought groceries. However, when I started to live with roommates in college and later with significant others, I learned that I constantly let food go to waste because I wasn't finishing it in a normal amount of time. People would joke with me and tell me that food "is meant to be eaten, not stored indefinitely," and I never really thought anything of it. But the more I think about it, I wonder if part of me still fears being without food and automatically stores it longer than I should. Again, it has been 16 years since I had to worry about missing a meal. Yet my body still reacts as if it was yesterday.

So, what does this mean? Well, what I take from this is that the effects of trauma don't just go away. Even after years of therapy, medication, and normalizing childhood experiences, the negative factors that shaped my life for so long still have a partial grip on me. I think people often assume that once children are removed from traumatizing experiences, they can start a healing process where one day they will be cured. What I am starting to understand is that it is more of a managing process and not a curing process. I have had to learn how to control my anxiety so that I can function in the world. I now know that conflict is something that I will struggle with because of my baseline anxiety level, so I will have to work on that. Now, I could go back to therapy, and I could start taking medication again, and maybe one day, I will. But for now, I plan to see if I can manage myself with the natural supports of my family and friends. I trust that if my situation ever becomes unmanageable, I have people who will not only help me realize it, but help me find the right resources. Every child that comes into care deserves to have that same kind of support system. Traumatized kids need people who will help them in the healing process while realizing that not everything can be "cured" in the traditional way we think about things. Sometimes simply having the awareness that a problem exists is enough to start working towards positive solutions and, in some cases, management.

As I begin the process of wrapping up this book and rereading over things, my mom, Lori, brought up an interesting point that I hadn't realized in the writing process (writing this book has led to lots of interesting discoveries). She pointed out that the thing that I seemed most concerned about in all that happened to my siblings and me was having enough to eat. We were being physically beaten on a pretty regular basis, yet the thing that I concerned myself with was getting food. In fact, the only reason why I ever told anyone what was going on at home was that I wanted one of my classmates to start bringing me extra food. There is just something about hunger that drives a person to do just about anything. Not just the physical hunger, but emotional hunger as well. The constant ache, the emptiness, the desperate need for nourishment, acknowledgement, love, and security is powerful. When such needs aren't met, nothing else seems to matter—not even massive negative or harmful actions or emotions. The hole, the missing pieces, take over everything—it's like nothing can make it across, around, or through the gap. As I've stated, I'm not sure that hole has been fully repaired. I'm not sure it can really be fixed. But in the process of learning how to manage it, letting the positive in a little at a time, I have reached a point where it's full enough most days. I think of it a bit like a major scar. Over time, the scar tissue fills in, but it's never quite flat, never quite normal. Recently I read somewhere that the scar tissue never fully replaces the damage but is actually stronger than the original cells. I don't know who I would have been if my life didn't include both the terror and the beauty of those early years. But deep inside, I do believe I am stronger for surviving them. And I intend to give that damaged-but-stronger part of myself in service to those who come after me so that perhaps, their scars won't have to be so deep.

A lot has happened to me in my 26 short years of living. As I look back on it all with nostalgia for the good times and a sense of triumph over the bad, I can't help but smile at all of the blessings that have been bestowed on me thus far. The joys and sorrows of the past have started to fade but allow me to remember where I came from and where I want to go. When I was little, I never imagined that I would be a person with a purpose in life, someone who gets to use his experiences to help make the world a better place. Even in writing this, I feel a surge of happiness as if I have been given some supernatural gift by which I must use my powers for the greater good. That is exactly what I plan to do. I will not allow the voices of others to be drowned out while the world continues to turn a blind eye.

There is a lot that I want to do and not a lot of time to do it in. And that's where the readers of this book come in. My challenge for anyone who has made it this far into the book is DO SOMETHING. Don't allow the words on these pages to bring about feelings of sadness and joy yet continue to live life ignoring the message. There are so many ways for people to get involved, and I encourage everyone to search within and figure out what that involvement may look like personally. Maybe you can be like Josh Niece or Susie and Zach Nettleton, who took me under their wings and mentored me: providing encouragement and sounding boards for the many troubles I was dealing with. Or maybe you have a passion to provide a forever family to a child in need, like Jack and Kaylee or my parents, Lori and Randy. Maybe you have the financial ability to allow foster children to have access to extracurricular activities, to aid them in finding their passion. With ever-dwindling support for those most at need, shoes and socks and backpacks—or Christmas and Birthday gifts—provide a real connection and a sense that someone out there cares. Whatever it is you have been gifted with, I ask you to consider using it for the betterment of children in need.

This is a call for guardian angels—for people who will stand up and say, "I care about the future of abused and neglected children." People who believe that every child matters and are willing to take a physical step to make this better. People who are tired of turning on the news and seeing another child who has died or another sibling group who has had to say goodbye to loved ones. It is time that we take a stand to protect one of our most valuable resources. If we are not taking care of these most vulnerable children, what kind of future are we setting up for ourselves?

I have been given so many wonderful opportunities in my life because of the love provided by family, therapists, friends, and many others. I want to see those same opportunities provided to all children. I want to wake up ten, fifteen, or twenty years from now and not have to say that I was one of the few "lucky ones." I want every child who goes through the foster care system to have safety and stability through permanency. I know what I have to do in order to make that dream a reality. While I know it's bold, I'm asking, what will you do?

WISDOM

The Quality or State of Being Wise; Knowledge of What Is True or Right Coupled with Just Judgment as to Action; Sagacity, Discernment or Insight

Final Thoughts

Massive mistakes were made in allowing our personal family situation to reach this extreme. Family, friends, teachers, administrators, state agencies, and the broader community all could have made different choices that might have prevented or lessened this catastrophe. Once it was all said and done, substantial efforts were made to cover-up and protect those who may have made mistakes, to diffuse blame and abdicate responsibility. From Mary and Tony's denial of responsibility to the organizations empowered to protect at-risk families, there was utter failures to ask simple questions and use common sense. Many mistakes were made, and abuses were covered over. One of the most deeply offensive issues occurred during the writing of this book. I spent the better part of a year trying to get access to my own files (court, counseling, and foster care system). After months of unreturned calls, lost files, and being told that it couldn't be done, I involved my mother, Lori Ross (a force of nature on her own). After some strategic calls, I did finally receive copies of my files. Thank you, Mom! Unfortunately, these files, though largely complete, had some very strategic missing pages, missing dates, "lost periods." I was required to sign documentation that prevents me from sharing those records, my records, with anyone. I cannot directly quote any part of the records.

Reviewing these files, reading through the challenges I put myself and everyone else through, understanding the depth of my issues, was difficult. I fiercely believe that everyone in this "system" deserves to have access to the story of his or her life. They deserve the opportunity to find out who they really are, what they really went through, once they reach adulthood. While I understand the desire of the system to "protect" itself, if the job of this behemoth is to protect at-risk families, then transparency and disclosure are essential. We cannot fix what we will not look at.

Perhaps the saddest thing about the foster care system, in its current state, is the number of children in this country who grow up without a forever family. A lot of times, these children are taken from the only families they have ever known and told by the State that they are going to have safety and stability in their lives. For many children, however, this is not the case. Some children will move between upwards of eight different homes in their very first year of being in foster care. That's eight different moms and dads, eight different sets of siblings, eight different attempts to learn the rules and fit in, and eight different bonds that are severed when the child moves. Would you keep trying after eight times? Other children are taken to residential treatment facilities where they are not to have any emotional connections with the staff, and instead of being treated like children who have survived trauma, they are treated like little criminals who need to be locked away. While these solutions might be physically safer for the children, what kind of adults are we creating?

So, between moving from foster home to foster home and/or living in residential treatment, these children have never learned what safety and stability is. Nor have they learned any of the socialization skills necessary for their proper integration into what we call "normal" society. Yet these children are released by the State at 18 or 21 years old and told to go out and become functioning members of society. So what happens to these children once they are released from the system? Unfortunately, many will fail to find adequate employment because they never finished high school, don't have proper transportation, and don't have anyone that they can call for guidance on what to do. These kids are expected to know everything about the adult world at 18 or 21 years old. I don't know about everyone else, but I certainly didn't have all the answers when I was 18 (even if I thought I did). Instead, I was able to call my mom or dad when I needed help and could rely on the fact that, for the most part, they could bail me out of any situation. For lots of these young adults, they quickly become homeless, incarcerated, or parents within their first two years on their own. And for some, they won't live to see their 30th birthday because of poor choices and bad circumstances. Think of how many times you relied on siblings, parents, friends, or co-workers, in your teens and early twenties. Now try to imagine the quality of your choices if none of these were available to you.

There has to be a better solution to protecting children. None of these options are acceptable. We as a society have to come to a point where we decide to care about the wellbeing of ALL of the people in our community, regardless of their socioeconomic status. We have to embrace our individualism but realize it only works if we all get through this together. My vision for the future is for all children who enter the foster care system to leave with the safety and stability provided by a forever family. EVERY single person in the world desires to have people they can turn to in times of need. EVERY person wants to be able to have a home to go to for the Holidays. And EVERY person deserves to have someone tell them that they are loved and cared for. It absolutely breaks my heart that there are children out there who will never hear someone tell them that they are loved unconditionally.

Therefore, I am calling for a nationwide change.

1. I want to see better policies in place for helping struggling families before they get to the point that they hurt or neglect a child(ren).
2. I want laws passed that allow child abuse and neglect investigators to assure children that they can talk about what is going on at home and will be protected from further harm

by the parent in question. Too many children fear talking to workers because they feel that even, and perhaps especially, if they say something, they will still have to go home and endure the abuse, or they fear the parents will be found innocent and the child will pay the consequences for telling.

3. I want laws that give parents limited chances to raise their children without abusing them. If a child is ever taken away because of severe abuse, that should be it, there is no redo; there is no second chance. It is time that we focus on the safety of the child and not the pleasing of the parents. I have seen too many stories where the parents have had their children taken away because of abuse, and because they completed some silly "steps program," the children were placed back in their care and sometime later, either the kids came into care again for the same reasons, or a worse fate had been dealt to them. This is simply unacceptable. No one should have to fear going home from school, waking up in the morning, or making noise in their house.

It is time that we as a society stand up and serve justice to those who commit crimes against their children, because that is exactly what they are doing, committing crimes. Parents need to be brought up on charges of child abuse and neglect and given sentences that fit the crimes committed. Now, I would never wish death on anyone—in fact, I feel the death penalty is the opposite of what Christ would want—but there should be real consequences that allow for the safety of the child and the monitored rehabilitation of the parents. Of course, many of these parents were themselves abused as children, and so they deserve the kind of assistance that can help them heal as they learn to become better parents. At the same time, parents need to be held more accountable for their actions, and they need to see that they live in a nation that cares about the wellbeing of ALL its members.

If the State decides that it is necessary to take a child from the custody of his parents, then it becomes the State's job to make sure that the child doesn't leave care until a permanent placement has been found that will provide safety, love, and stability. In my vision for the future, it will no longer be acceptable for a child to "age out" of the system. Instead, the very first day that a child enters care, someone will take charge of that child's life and make sure that the best possible outcome is found. It is a personal goal of mine to make sure that every child feels the love and support that I felt from my resource team. Unfortunately, I know this is not the norm. If I were personally charged with the task of improving the system, here are a few of the steps I'd attempt.

1. No child will be viewed, on any level, as a case number but as a wonderful, complex human being in need of love and support.

2. No longer will some children in foster care get maximum attention from social workers while others spend their entire time in the system without even knowing their worker's name. Every child deserves the very best we can deliver. Period.

3. Each child entering care will be given access to every resource necessary for the proper development of that child. That means access to quality therapists, mentors, parent-aids, Guardians Ad Litem, CASA workers, caseworkers, adoption specialists, foster and adoptive parents, and the list goes on and on.

4. All of those resources (from caseworkers to judges) and any others involved will have a deep and comprehensive understanding of all of the issues and challenges involved in a specific child's life, so that informed decisions can be made in the best interests of the child. Sending challenged and challenging foster children to unprepared foster homes serves no one. Failures in adult communication all too often result in further traumatization of children in care.

5. The unique needs, story, and voice of every child in care are cherished and preserved and, when age appropriate, each child is given full access to their story in an environment that supports their understanding of the information.

6. Children will not be placed in multiple foster homes or residential facilities where they feel like criminals.
7. Children should know the names of their support team members and the support team members should know the names of each child.
8. Finally, if a child is moved into an adoptive home but still requires services, those services will be continued until the child no longer needs them. It is unacceptable for the State to decide that services should stop, and the responsibility should solely fall on the shoulders of the parents. We do not get to stop caring about the wellbeing of children at any point in time. Instead, we as a society have to decide to provide our full support in any way that we can.

So, how do we go about getting these much-needed changes?

I think the first thing we have to decide, as a society, is that this country wasn't built by people saying, "It's not my problem," but instead, by people imagining a better way and trying to work every day towards that better vision. Some of those attempts succeed, some fail, but each day we try, progress is made. The next thing I think is essential is that we do what we say we believe. We need people that will stand before legislators and demand a government that cares about its children. We need people that will find solutions. We need people who will actually do something to make it better.

What can you do specifically? Not everyone is a therapist or is meant to be a foster or adoptive parent, but everyone can make a difference.

Consider the following:

1. Advocate for the children in need in your community
2. Vote to support those unable to protect themselves
3. Spread the word about the needs of children to family, friends, co-workers

4. Donate to charitable organizations (please do your own research on the efficacy and validity of these entities) that serve children and families in need

5. If you have the ability to do more, then:

    a. Become a mentor to a child in care.

    b. Become a foster family.

    c. Adopt a child or children in need and provide them with a forever family.

Whatever it is, DO SOMETHING!! Everyone has something that they can do, some resource that they can provide that can help out a child in need. We all have something that we can give to a child to let them know that the storm is temporary, and that morning will come. I know we have our work cut out for us, but I also believe that if we work hard enough, there will be real and positive changes in the lives of children who would otherwise have no hope. So, I thank you all. Each person that has decided to step up and make a difference in their community. People like you who decided to care about the path my life took, saved me, and I couldn't be more grateful.

Many blessings, friends. I look forward to seeing the wonderful world that is shaped by the actions of champions.

TIMELINE OF EVENTS

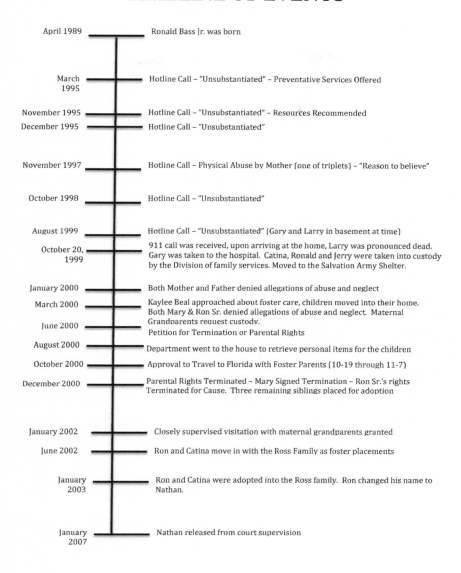

April 1989	Ronald Bass Jr. was born
March 1995	Hotline Call – "Unsubstantiated" – Preventative Services Offered
November 1995	Hotline Call – "Unsubstantiated" – Resources Recommended
December 1995	Hotline Call – "Unsubstantiated"
November 1997	Hotline Call – Physical Abuse by Mother (one of triplets) – "Reason to believe"
October 1998	Hotline Call – "Unsubstantiated"
August 1999	Hotline Call – "Unsubstantiated" (Gary and Larry in basement at time)
October 20, 1999	911 call was received, upon arriving at the home, Larry was pronounced dead. Gary was taken to the hospital. Catina, Ronald and Jerry were taken into custody by the Division of family services. Moved to the Salvation Army Shelter.
January 2000	Both Mother and Father denied allegations of abuse and neglect
March 2000	Kaylee Beal approached about foster care, children moved into their home. Both Mary & Ron Sr. denied allegations of abuse and neglect. Maternal Grandparents request custody.
June 2000	Petition for Termination or Parental Rights
August 2000	Department went to the house to retrieve personal items for the children
October 2000	Approval to Travel to Florida with Foster Parents (10-19 through 11-7)
December 2000	Parental Rights Terminated – Mary Signed Termination – Ron Sr.'s rights Terminated for Cause. Three remaining siblings placed for adoption
January 2002	Closely supervised visitation with maternal grandparents granted
June 2002	Ron and Catina move in with the Ross Family as foster placements
January 2003	Ron and Catina were adopted into the Ross family. Ron changed his name to Nathan.
January 2007	Nathan released from court supervision

191

RESOURCES

Child Abuse

- If you witness a child needing immediate help, call 911. If you suspect that a child is being abused, contact Childhelp the National Child Abuse Hotline at 1-800-422-4453 (1-800-4-A-Child), or you can reach them on the web at http://www.childwelfare.gov/responding
- National Children's Alliance accredits Child Advocacy Centers in many communities. For a list of accredited organizations, go to http://www.nationalchildrensalliance.org
- National Parent Helpline
- US Department of Health and Human Services, Administration for Children and Families
- US Department of Justice, Office of Juvenile Justice and Delinquency Prevention
- Prevent Child Abuse America
- National Center for Missing & Exploited Children
- American Academy of Pediatrics
- The Child Abuse Prevention Network
- National Children's Advocacy Center
- American Professional Society on the Abuse of Children
- First Witness Child Abuse Resource Center
- International Justice Mission
- Child Welfare Information Gateway
- Child Trauma Academy
- Kempe Foundation for the Prevention of Child Abuse and Neglect
- National Children's Alliance

NOTES

[i] "Starved and Scalded, 8-year-old Brothers Die", Kansas City Star, 24 Oct 1999.

[ii] "Police look into the death of triplets", Lubbock Avalanche-Journal, 23 October 19999 (Referenced Associate Press).

[iii] "Man pleads guilty in abuse case", Kansas City Star, Joe Lambe, 26 January 2001.

[iv] D. Scott Forrester, conservator for the estate of Jerry Bass v. Mary Bass, Tony Dixon, Defendants, Kimberly Rosa, Melissa Johnson, Appellants., No. 04-1923, United States Court of Appeals, Eighth Circuit, Submitted: 18 Nov 2004, Filed: 7 Feb 2005.

[v] Two out of three triplets died from abuse", Associated Press, Craig Horst, 23 October 1999.

[vi] D. Scott Forrester, conservator for the estate of Jerry Bass v. Mary Bass, Tony Dixon, Defendants, Kimberly Rosa, Melissa Johnson, Appellants., No. 04-1923, United States Court of Appeals, Eighth Circuit, Submitted: 18 Nov 2004, Filed: 7 Feb 2005.

[vii] D. Scott Forrester, conservator for the estate of Jerry Bass v. Mary Bass, Tony Dixon, Defendants, Kimberly Rosa, Melissa Johnson, Appellants., No. 04-1923, United States Court of Appeals, Eighth Circuit, Submitted: 18 Nov 2004, Filed: 7 Feb 2005.

[viii] "Child Maltreatment 2010", US Department of Health & Human Services, Administration for Children and Families, Administration on Children, Youth and Families, Children's Bureau, 2010.

[ix] "Child Maltreatment 2010", US Department of Health & Human Services, Administration for Children and Families, Administration on Children, Youth and Families, Children's Bureau, 2010.

x "Child Maltreatment 2010", US Department of Health & Human Services, Administration for Children and Families, Administration on Children, Youth and Families, Children's Bureau, 2010.

xi "Data Snapshot on Foster Care Placement", datacenter.kidscount.org, Annie E. Casey Foundation. May 2011

xii "Trends in Foster Care and Adoption – FY 2002-FY 2011" Children's Bureau, US Department of Health and Human Services, Administration for Children and Families, Administration on Children, Youth and Families, 12 July 2012. www.acf.hhs.gov/programs/cb

xiii "Children in Public Foster Care on September 30th of each year who are waiting to be adopted. FY 2002-FY 2011" Children's Bureau, US Department of Health and Human Services, Administration for Children and Families, Administration on Children, Youth and Families, 12 July 2012. www.acf.hhs.gov/programs/cb

xiv Adoption History in Brief, The Adoption History Project, darkwing.uoregon.edu.

xv Facts and Statistics, Congressional Coalition on Adoption Institute, www.ccainstitute.org

Made in the USA
Coppell, TX
27 January 2020

15055456R00118